OPENING FORBIDDEN LAKES

Let's open 'em all!

Fishing Colorado's Watersheds—
Without Getting Arrested

by

Zoltan Malocsay

Squeezy Press

Library of Congress Catalog Card Number
CIP 92-61259

ISBN: 0-9629250-1-2

Cover design by Dolores Arnold

Cover photo by Charles Lamoreaux

Cartoon published with permission of the artist:
Ken Keegan

First Edition
Printed in the United States of America

Published by
Squeezy Press
P.O. Box 60412
Colorado Springs, CO 80906-2455

Outdoor sports have inherent dangers and no guide can
substitute for sound judgement. Good decision-making is
the responsibility of the individual. Do not trespass.

This is for George Whitley of the Isaac Walton League and Trout Unlimited, who argued so forcefully for the opening of forbidden lakes, all the while knowing that he would not live to fish beside us when they opened.

"In the West, whiskey's for drinkin' and water's for fightin'."
—Mark Twain

TABLE OF CONTENTS

AUTHOR'S NOTE

Many of our most popular fishing lakes are drinking water reservoirs for Colorado's front range cities. Good fishing and good water quality go together. So why are other lakes in the same systems closed to public fishing?

This book has three aims: First, a detailed fishing guide to the wonderful reservoirs already open (most are open now and more are opening each year), and second, to show you what we're all missing at their sister lakes, the forbidden lakes, public drinking water still closed to the public that owns it. (Despite the best in modern water treatment.)

Once you see the whole set—open and closed alike—keeping part of it locked seems tragically unnecessary. Especially when you discover that fishing and fish management are actually good for our lakes, that fish management improves and helps safeguard them. Indeed, fishing is such a good idea that all new reservoirs are built open: Only the oldest lakes are closed under old rules.

That's how we come to my third aim and why we include a unique last chapter to "put a lake opener in your pocket." You see, reservoirs don't open themselves. Some have been shut since 1913, and if you want them open, you need to understand the argument, the reasoning, the excuses, so you can encourage your local officials with solid information instead of empty complaints.

You need to know what's going on.

For generations anglers have wondered and grumbled, yearning to know what goes on behind the "No Trespassing" signs and the locked gates guarding our watersheds. Rumors rage about forbidden lakes being enjoyed by a privileged few or an illegal legion. Local fishermen sneak in and wind up getting tickets, prosecuted by the same governments that spend taxpayers' money trying to lure tourist fishermen to other drinking water reservoirs.

Does this make sense to you?

Maybe not, but fortunately, it's time to celebrate a shift in history, for "No Trespassing" signs are beginning to fall like dominoes up and down the front range. A word from you might topple the next one.

Meanwhile, there are lots of great lakes already open and lots of ways to enjoy them, so this book is packed with fun—and with details. Here you'll get details about water ecology, stocking and fish census information (what kinds, how many, how big and how they're doing) road directions, best spots, best techniques, special rules, boat ramps, shoreline trails, camping, everything knowable from the fish biology to stories by other fishermen.

Open or closed, our drinking water lakes certainly do have the fish and the scenery that made Colorado famous. And they are certainly owned by the public. We don't cover lakes owned by individuals or corporations or federal lakes used to transfer water, but we welcome your suggestions for lakes to be included in future editions.

As the author of the *Trails Guide to Pikes Peak Country*, it always burned me up that I could explore a million acres of the Pike National Forest extending across five counties, but was locked away from most of Pikes Peak itself. America's most famous mountain has five watersheds belonging to four cities, so the public is only welcome on strips and pieces of a mountain that symbolized America's hope and freedom to the Pikes Peak or Bust pioneers. Surely, it was the peak's "purple mountain majesty" that inspired the words to the song *America the Beautiful*, not all those "No Trespassing" signs!

For me, the situation turned around when the tallies showed that most of our front range reservoirs are now open as of 1992. Denver and other Colorado cities are on their way to doing what Aurora did in 1991, opening everything. Colorado Springs opened three more in 1992.

This book is the culmination of more than a decade of personal involvement, and I hope it charges your batteries the way it does mine.

—Zoltan

ACKNOWLEDGMENTS

Nobody helped at all except the following army of authorities and anglers who tried their best to keep me from fouling up the facts. Very special thanks go to two Division of Wildlife biologists, Douglas Krieger and Greg Policky, who never shrank under my barrage of questions. But despite all this help and review, the opinions expressed in this book are my own and do not necessarily reflect the views and policies of my sources. Indeed, some chose not to be named.

Colorado Division of Wildlife: Douglas Krieger, Greg Policky, Phil Goebel, Jim Satterfield, John Torres, Clee Sealing, Jake Bennett, Dave Clippinger, Eric Lundberg, Mark Elkins.

Denver Water Board: Bob Taylor, Michele Radice, Hamlet "Chips" Barry III, Chuck Smith, Ed Christiansen.

Aurora: Pete Smith, Rick Mueller, Milton Hunholz.

Boulder: Robert E. Williams and Joseph N. deRaismes III.

Palmer Lake: Bob Radosevich, Mike Kazeck, Jill Simpson, Bob Schroeder.

Colorado Springs: Vic Ecklund, Don Mulligan, Bill Stookey, Jim Rees, Paul Butcher, Tom Gayler, Mike Madonna.

Manitou Springs: Dan Wecks, Johnnie Price, Larry Manning.

Cripple Creek: Charlie Houghton, Chip Huffman, Jerry Whiteman.

Victor: Carl Roy, Sandy MacDougall, Ken Geddes, P.J. Anderson.

Plus anglers Denny O'Connor, Greg Kelley, Sandy Kraemer, Charles Lamoreaux, Stuart Dodge, Norman Benson, Rick Romero.

Also, **U.S. Fish and Wildlife** Biologist Bruce Rosenlund and Mike Babler of the **U.S. Air Force Academy**, John Scherschligt of the State Health Dept., and Jim Montoya, Ken Marler and Royce McCrary of the **Forest Service**.

ABOUT THE AUTHOR

Zoltan Malocsay has been prying open reservoirs with his mouth for the past dozen years. As the author of a popular trails guide, he has a working relationship with officials of many local, state and federal agencies. A decade ago, Zoltan was elected chairman of a broadly-based citizens group called the Pikes Peak Committee for Freer Use of Public Lands and helped negotiate the opening of Penrose-Rosemont Reservoir.

Encouraged by that success, Zoltan lobbied for the opening of more reservoirs. In 1991, the Colorado Springs City Council appointed him to its North Slope Watershed Advisory Committee, and members elected him vice chairman. That committee worked out details for the 1992 opening three of the largest reservoirs on Pikes Peak: Crystal, South Catamount and North Catamount.

Zoltan is also the author of a novel, *Galloping Wind*, published by Putnam and by Dell, and has published 14 short stories in Boy's Life Magazine. He is also a jewelry designer whose line of 14k jewelry is sold to retail stores throughout much of the United States and Barbados and the Bahamas.

ABOUT THE OTHERS:

All sorts of citizens have doubtless worked behind the scenes to help open forbidden lakes, but here are a few that we know of:

Peak Area Recreation Concept (Jaycee sponsored): Sandy Kraemer, chairman; Frederich Reich, David Guevara.

Pikes Peak Committee for Freer Use of Public Lands: Zoltan Malocsay, chairman; George Whitley, A.H. McElhany, Polly Parent, Bob Ormes, James Langran, Tom Haggard, Marilyn Hinterberger, Gary Lee, Bill Dudley, Lucia Menges.

North Slope Watershed Advisory Committee: Stuart Dodge, chairman; Zoltan Malocsay, vice chairman; Gregory Kelley, Larry Grimaldi, James Strub, Denver Bolster, Richard Bratton, Sandy Kraemer, Lee Milner, Norman Benson, Judith Daley, Harold Heyse, Tracy Kissler, Harlan Nimrod, Brooke Smith, Thomas Papadinoff and Bud Owsley.

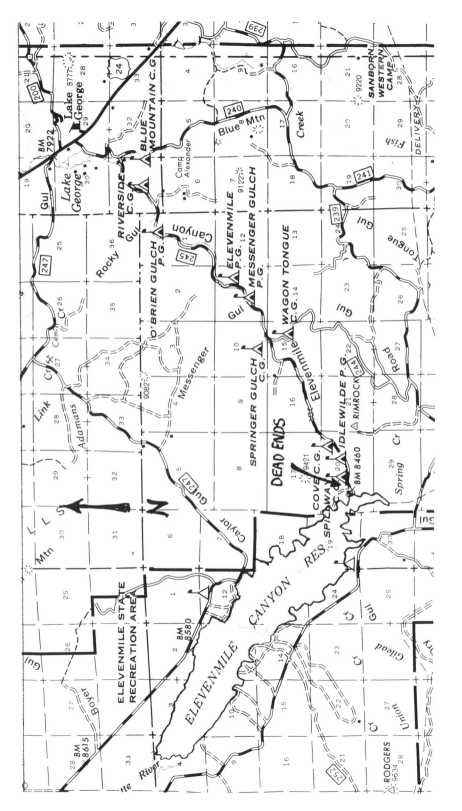

DENVER WATER BOARD LAKES
8 Open to All
6 Still Closed to All

Elevenmile Canyon Reservoir (Open)
Antero Reservoir (Open)
Williams Fork Reservoir (Open)
Gross Reservoir (Open)
Lake Cheesman (Open)
Strontia Springs Reservoir (Open)
Lake Dillon (Open)
Piney Lake (Open)
Ralston Reservoir (Closed)
Long Lakes (Both Closed)
Marston Reservoir (Closed)
Harriman Reservoir (Closed)
Platte Canyon Reservoir (Closed)

"It is no longer acceptable to say, 'We only do water'," says the newly appointed manager of the Denver Water Board, Hamlet "Chips" Barry III. "Our charter directs us to provide water for Denver, so that has to remain primary, but we are also in the recreation business, whether we like it or not. We have a responsibility to provide more recreation in our watersheds."

With a long career in natural resource law and management, most recently as director of the Colorado Department of Natural Resources, Barry has set out to improve the DWB's image with fishermen and conservationists. His appointment came only four days after the Environmental Protection Agency vetoed the controversial Two Forks Dam Proposal.

Yet even before Barry's appointment, the experimental opening of Cheesman Reservoir was considered a guarded success and did much to encourage the search for more fishing opportunities.

Most of Denver's water is already open, but six reservoirs remain closed, and we'll describe them all as part of the total system. Each has its own problems and qualities, so we'll explore their possibilities in detail.

But despite all the optimism, there are some major problems. Unlike other water departments that are city controlled, the Denver Water Board is entirely separate from the City of Denver, so the Denver City Council cannot direct city departments such as Parks and Recreation to carry out DWB plans. They try to work together closely, but things just aren't as automatic as they are in other area governments.

Even worse, the DWB's pro-recreation philosophy comes without a budget to back it up. The charter which created the DWB was not designed to put the water department into the recreation business, and some Denver residents who are already unhappy about their water bills threaten to sue if rate-payers' money is spent on recreation. So the DWB will need help from other agencies and perhaps private concessionaires to develop more recreation.

Still, the department is exploring its options. Barry has appointed a five-member committee to draft a policy guideline for recreation uses of water department properties. His staff has come up with a shopping list of fishing projects and proposals to solve problems at particular sites. They include consideration of opening closed reservoirs, agreements to exchange water with Aurora to help regulate flows in South Park and a deal to sell prime river fishing properties to the DOW.

The Aurora agreement should benefit both Antero and Spinney Mountain Reservoirs and the South Platte River below them. If Aurora stores all the water it needs in Spinney, the flow below it could be reduced enough to harm fishing. So Denver may store Aurora's water in Cheesman, which should help stabilize flows. Denver also needs to drain Antero long enough to repair the dam and its outlet, so Spinney may be able to store Antero's water temporarily.

In Middle Park the DWB owns prize river fishing properties that will be sold to the Division of Wildlife. This includes about one and a half miles of the Williams Fork River below the Williams Fork Reservoir and another two miles of the main-stem Colorado River just below its confluence with the Williams Fork. These waters are excellent habitat and feature brown and rainbow trout, averaging 14 to 16 inches and weighing up to five pounds.

The properties involved are known as the Kemp Ranch, 1,778 acres, and the Corral Creek Ranch, 590 acres. The Colorado Legislature has already approved the deal, so the DOW is proceeding to buy the ranches with money raised from fishing licenses.

And there's more. The veto of Two Forks means that the DWB won't need that stretch of closed water along the South Fork of the North Platte near Pine, so Jefferson County Open Space is now developing an elaborate park there. The park also includes a sizable lake with good fishing potential. Jefferson County always builds excellent facilities, so the work probably can't be completed until 1993 or later. But however long it takes, the new park promises to be a quality recreational site, despite the fact that this particular stretch of river is not as rich.

All in all, the giant water system that feeds Denver is poised to offer more and more recreation in coming years. But as you'll see, past efforts have resulted in most of that system being open to anglers right now.

Let's start with the system's biggest and most productive lake first:

ELEVENMILE CANYON RESERVOIR, 3,405 surface acres, deepest point 115 ft., altitude 8,620 ft., built in 1932.

ROAD DIRECTIONS: To find ELEVENMILE RESERVOIR, take I-25 south to Colorado Springs and take the Manitou-Pikes Peak Exit 141, which puts you heading west on Hwy. 24. Drive to Lake George. YOU CANNOT REACH THE RESERVOIR DIRECTLY VIA ELEVEN-MILE CANYON ROAD AT LAKE GEORGE. This scenic gravel road offers popular roadside river fishing, but dead ends below the dam. The only way to use it to access the reservoir is by turning left off the canyon road at Wagon Tongue Campground (#244), then right onto

#239, then right onto Ranger Station Gulch Road and that will take you to the Witcher's Cove area. However, I wouldn't drag a big boat over this route, and the entire Elevenmile Canyon gets so much use that authorities have proposed closing it to motor vehicle traffic, making it a hike-in or bicycle-in fishing area.

The best way to reach ELEVENMILE RESERVOIR *is to take the next left on the west edge of Lake George. Look for a small sign on your left where the river crosses the road. This is #247, Caylor Gulch Road, but notice the odd, tiny Y intersection there at Hwy. 24. If you're dragging a heavy boat, be sure to pass up the first leg of that Y, instead crossing the river on the highway, and take the second leg of the Y. That's because the first (east) leg has its own little bridge, and it's not very strong. Once on this road, bear left at the next intersection, ignoring #249 to Wilkerson Pass, and you'll find the lake. What we call the main boat ramp is to the right.*

"Elevenmile is one of the most productive lakes on the front range," says DOW Biologist Douglas Krieger. "Just like in your garden, rich alkaline soils produce lots of nutrients to grow plants, which grows a lot of bugs, and that's why the fish grow so fast."

Elevenmile is Denver's biggest reservoir and has long been a favorite among anglers who like to eat fish because it produces so many nice stringers. Your average rainbow will run between 12 and 16 inches. Indeed, a lot of anglers report that they don't catch any below 14 inches, and the larger ones run to 32 inches. So **there is a special limit on trout: eight fish, but only two can be longer than 16 inches.** There are not many browns, but you have your best chance of catching them at night or while ice fishing. The Denver Water Board keeps Elevenmile pretty full, so **ice fishing is permitted and it's great.**

"I'd pit Elevenmile against any kokanee lake in the state," Krieger said. "Both the size and numbers are good, so we don't really know how many the lake can support. To find that out, we've been stocking about a million a year for several years now. We'll know when we've reached the maximum when adults mature to smaller sizes. That's how we work out the optimum level."

Salmon venture near shore when the ice melts in spring, especially at the west end. After that, they go to deep water, primarily the old river channel, and you'll find them about another half mile farther down each week. Try trolling with a short silver Rapala faster than you think you should.

In late June there's a damsel fly hatch, so kokanee come to the shallows to feed. That's a good time to catch them with flies. Caught that way, kokanee are famous, tail-walking fighters. Otherwise, they stay very deep through July and August.

Once they're about two years old, salmon are safe from most pike. Male salmon mature in three years, females in four, then they attempt to spawn and die. Their instinct is to swim back to the stream where they hatched, but since they were delivered by truck, each fall large numbers show up at the bank looking for that truck. What they find is a swarm of anglers, raking the water with snag hooks. It's an impressive harvest.

But here's a tip for fly fishermen. It is a myth that kokanee don't bite white spawning. "Use an egg pattern fly when they come in close," says DOW Biologist Greg Policky. "That's fun."

Back in the early 60's, Elevenmile had about 100 suckers for every trout, so the DOW introduced northern pike to control the suckers and carp. That worked, but eventually the pike population exploded. "It was out of control for awhile," Krieger said.

The situation has since stabilized, but **there are still too many small pike in the weedy shallows that rim most of the lake.** Trout fishermen lose a lot of flies and lures to these sharp-toothed hammer handles, and you have to fish deeper water to avoid them. Bank fishermen can often avoid them by casting from the rocks toward the west end of the north shore.

Too many pike make Elevenmile expensive to stock because they eat so many trout. The DOW tries to get around this by stocking larger trout, 7-inch rainbows and cutthroats. (The Snake River cutthroats now seem to be spawning in the river above.)

"We'd like to encourage anglers to eat more small pike instead of releasing them," Krieger advised. "They're exceptional eating, especially baked as fillets. The forked bones make them tricky to fillet, but once you get it down, they're pretty easy. Your bag limit is 20, so please take plenty!"

The division would like to see fewer and larger pike because **big pike are cannibals, so they will eventually control their**

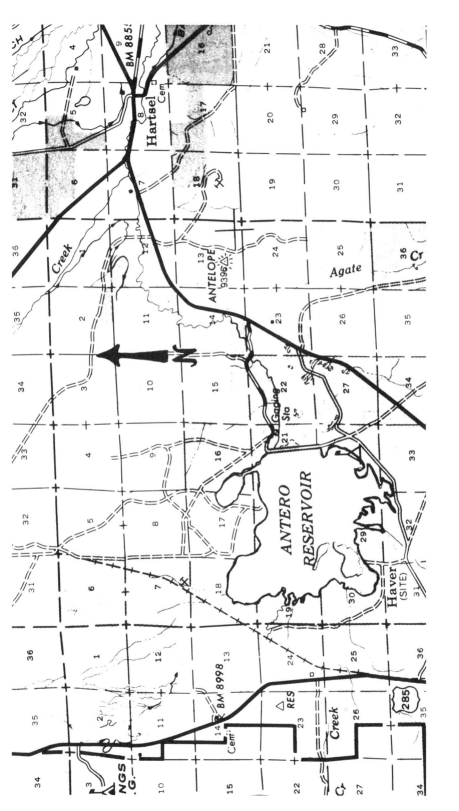

own **numbers,** just as they do at Spinney. A special slot limit may soon help with that.

Of course, Elevenmile also has a few good-sized brookies, but lake trout are no longer stocked because, as Krieger told us, "We don't want any more teeth in the lake."

A day fee is required, $3 per car, and the Colorado Division of Parks and Outdoor Recreation manages 12 rather primitive campgrounds around the lake, some of which operate year round ($6 per night per unit). There are no hookups, but all now have hand-pump potable water. Restrooms are vault type. There are three adequate boat ramps, barely two abreast, two on the north side and one on the south side. Courtesy docks are provided at all three ramps.

What we call the main ramp near the entrance from Lake George is just a little short for big boats. Your trailer tires nearly come off the end of the concrete before a big boat floats, so as soon as it does float, stop! The parking lot ahead is also very level, so as you back up, the boat suddenly dips out of sight as it starts down the ramp.

ANTERO RESERVOIR, 2,111 surface acres, deepest point26 ft., elevation 8,940 ft., built in 1909.

ROAD DIRECTIONS: ANTERO is located less than 20 miles south of Fairplay off Hwy 285 from Denver or about six miles west of Hartsel off Hwy 24 from Colorado Springs. There are a number of small access roads leading from the highways.

Cross a female lake trout with a male brook trout and you have a splake, a fish that is considered "vulnerable to fishing with a high catch rate," as biologists put it. Introduced in 1990, Antero's splake have already reached 15 inches and are doing better than rainbows ever did.

Yet the big news is that Antero's two major problems may be solved in coming years. Like other South Park lakes, Antero is a great producer, but is much shallower than the others. It's catch rate is higher than Elevenmile's, but fish tend to be smaller because they compete with a lot of suckers for food.

Imagine how good Antero could be if it were deeper and

had fewer suckers. That may happen because the DWB is proposing repairs that will deepen the lake. That work will require draining it for as much as a year, giving the DOW a chance to remove suckers.. (They'll be back, eventually coming in from above.) The only hitch is that no date has yet been set, but it is part of the five-year plan.

Antero was built over the site of a smaller lake called Green Lake, and the older lake's bottom is a good place to fish. It lies on the northwest corner of Antero and comes closest to the bank on the north at Rainbow point. Ice fishing is exceptional.

Since the splake are new, Antero's mainstay is still put-and-take rainbows from 10 to 14 inches. The lake is no longer stocked with kokanee, but it still has a few (about one salmon for every 50 trout). Oddly enough, Antero's salmon actually manage to reproduce, spawning in the inlet.

The DOW itself manages recreation here, so everything is free and easy-going, but very primitive. Restrooms are only outhouses, and there are no picnic facilities. You can park just about any place, and you are welcome to camp, but you must be self-contained because there are no services and there is no potable water.

Like its sister lakes in South Park, Antero lies in a grassy bowl with mountains in the distance all around. No trees. Bring your hat and sunscreen and insect repellent and something to drink. This treeless landscape also makes Antero subject to strong winds, so boaters have to watch the sky. There can be quite a huddle when everybody decides to get off the lake at the same time. It's only boat ramp is concrete and adequate, but only two abreast.

Belly boating is very popular. I've seen Antero look like a frying vat at Dunkin' Donuts, but no boating or tubing is permitted between 9 p.m. and 4 a.m.

There is no public access to the west face of the dam, nor along the south and west shoreline because of private property. But watch the news because the DOW is busy acquiring stream rights in the area. The Badger Basin Ranch on the south and middle forks near Hartsel extends to within a mile below Antero, and should add a total of 18 miles of great river fishing. In addition, the DWB is buying the 63 Ranch above Antero for the Antero expansion and will sell the DOW an easement to about four miles of the unflooded river there.

For a description of Spinney Reservoir, see Aurora.

WILLIAMS FORK RESERVOIR, 1,860 surface acres, deepest part 168 ft., altitude 7,800 ft., completed in 1959.

ROAD DIRECTIONS: To find WILLIAMS FORK RESERVOIR from Denver, head west on I-70, take the US 40 exit for Berthoud Pass and Winter Park. Stay on 40 past Granby and four miles west of Hot Sulphur Springs, turn left onto the access road. From Colorado Springs, take Hwy. 24 west, then past Hartsel take Hwy 9 to Frisco and pick up I-70 east briefly to the Silverthorn Exit. Head north again on Hwy 9 to Kremmling, then east on US 40. Much of this stretch from Silverthorn past Parshall is Gold Medal stream fishing along the Blue and Colorado Rivers. Three quarters of a mile past Parshall, turn right onto the access road.

Williams Fork Reservoir has new concrete boat ramps for 1992. The Denver Water Board, which manages recreation here, replaced the old gravel ramps with two concrete ramps, one on each side of the lake. A rare spring draw-down was required for this effort, but the new ramps should be useable even when the lake is low. They measure about 21 feet wide by 230 feet long.

Surrounded by sagebrush, Williams Fork offers good rainbow and kokanee fishing. Some 50,000 to 70,000 catchable rainbows are stocked each year in May and June and grow fat because of the lake's rich plankton supply. Creel census reports show that fishermen catch 13 to 15-inch rainbows. Ice fishermen often catch bigger trout.

DOW Fish Biologist Jake Bennett says the kokanee fishing is the best ever at Williams Fork. Some 300,000 are stocked each year and grow to 14 inches at spawning. But a lot of trollers catch two-year-old kokanee averaging about 11 inches by trolling in July and August, especially when wind puts a little chop on the water. If it's calm, the salmon don't seem to bite. Bennett recommends trolling a Triple Teaser along the old channel towards the inlet near the east boat ramp.

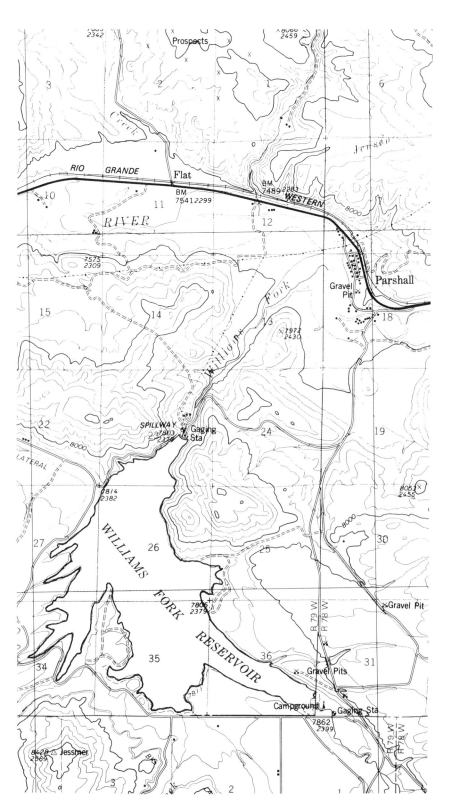

This is not a brown trout lake. An occasional brown is caught, which keeps the dream alive, but gill net samplings almost never turn up any.

Northern pike have managed the sucker problem, but northerns have been hammered lately, so it would be a good idea for awhile to release the northerns you catch here.

The slot limit on lake trout has been removed, but not because lakers are doing so well. Just the opposite. Mackinaw never really took off as they should have at Williams Fork, and biologists are beginning to think the original plant was not well suited. So you are welcome to harvest the usual limit of lake trout, if you can, because the DOW wants to start over with lakers from a different source.

Originally, this lake was supposed to be managed by the state, but there was a problem, and the Federal Energy Regulatory Commission threatened to yank its permit if there wasn't more recreation. The Denver Water Board had to take over recreational operation and the DWB continues operations today. There are no services, but fishing, boating and camping are all free.

GROSS RESERVOIR, 440 surface acres, deepest part296 ft. altitude 7,285 ft., completed in 1954.

ROAD DIRECTIONS: To find Gross Reservoir, take Colorado Hwy 72 some 35 miles northwest of Denver to approximately one mile east of Wondervu, then head north on the reservoir access road for 4 miles. From Boulder, take Flagstaff Mountain Road 12 miles southwest to the east side of Gross.

Like Cheesman, the issue at Gross Reservoir is boating. The winds are too nasty for car-top boats, so gasoline boats would be safer. Indeed, there is no particular opposition to boating or gasoline at Gross, but engineers are puzzled about the problem of building a bring-your-own-boat ramp. Fluctuating levels would require a very long ramp, and the underwater topography demands that it be very steep, which can make it difficult to haul a boat out.

"Unless we can find a concessionaire that could operate boats

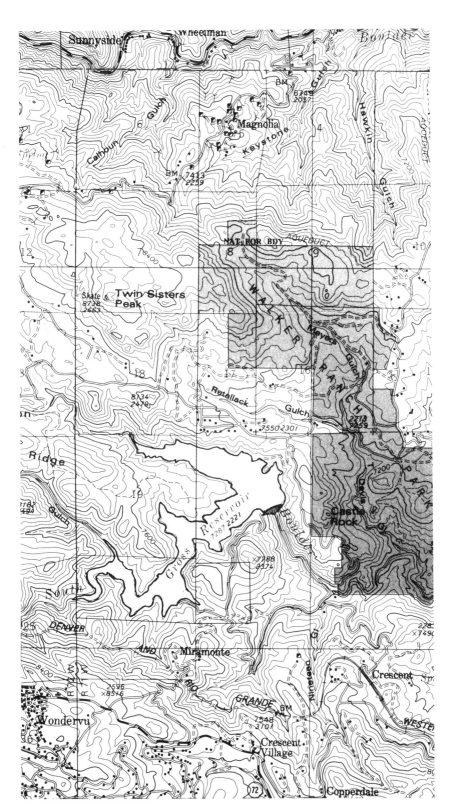

from a floating dock, it's going to be very expensive to have boating at Gross," says Bob Taylor, DWB Environmental Coordinator.

Despite the fluctuating levels, however, Gross offers some good fishing. Catchable rainbow are its mainstay and some of the carry-overs grow large. It also has good yellow perch and some tiger muskie available from its rocky shore, but because it was built in canyon, bank fishing is difficult. And since the shoreline measures 10.9 miles, you can imagine how hard it is to scramble very far in this day-use area.

The boating issue is also important because Gross has good kokanee and some lake trout, both of which like to stay deep most of the summer.

No fishing is permitted from 9 p.m. to 4 a.m. No camping is allowed. Fires must be in established firepits on the north side. Kokanee snagging is permitted from Sept. 1 to Jan. 31.

CHEESMAN RESERVOIR, 874 surface acres, deepest part197 ft., elevation 6,842 ft., completed 1905.

ROAD DIRECTIONS: Distance from Denver: 60 miles. From Denver take Hwy. 285 south to Pine Junction, then head south on 126 to Deckers. From Colorado Springs, take Hwy. 24 west to Woodland Park, then right on 67 to Deckers. To find CHEESMAN, take the Cheesman turnoff (#211) 2.7 miles west of Deckers and follow the signs 3.2 miles to the lake. Park outside the fence. As you enter the gate, SHORELINE TRAIL is immediately on your right. CHEESMAN DAM TRAIL is straight ahead, but you must walk roads to reach it, so see its trail description for directions.

Sparkling water rippling beside the highway near Deckers lures many people to pull over and fly fish those sections of the South Fork of the South Platte open to the public (limit: two trout over 16;" flies and lures only). And Gill Trail, just 1/10th of a mile east of the Cheesman turnoff on 126, offers Gold Medal catch-and-release fishing going upstream along the Platte. If you keep hiking Gill upstream until the trail vanishes amid the cliffs and boulders, you discover a curving granite wall that looks like something the Incas might have constructed.

Cheesman Dam is made of giant blocks of the same granite

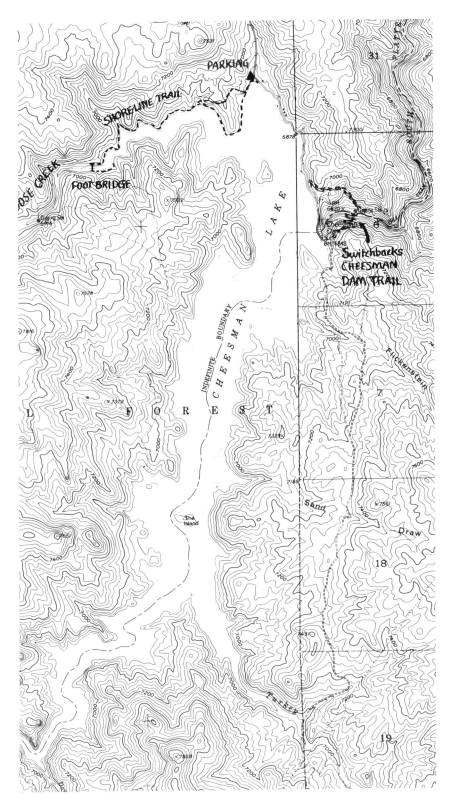

that forms the cliffs, and beyond it lies Denver's most beautiful reservoir. Cheesman should also be one of Denver's best fishing lakes, but right now the DOW cannot stock it as they wish because the fish would be largely wasted.

You see, Cheesman is best suited for lake trout and kokanee, but those fish run deep and require boats for successful angling. In fact, even the lake's smallmouth bass, northern pike, yellow perch and rainbows and browns would be easier to reach by boat because Cheesman's steep and rugged banks are hard to fish.

In fall, lower levels create some stretches of sandy gravel beach, but even these are interrupted by rock formations. And since no boats or floatation devices are allowed, this means scrambling treacherous terrain. **So why aren't boats allowed?**

Officials say that Cheesman is not the kind of lake where you can run to shore when chinooks blow down the canyon. You can't beach a boat in most places. This means that gasoline boats, such as those used by authorities, would be the safest answer, and the DWB does not object to gasoline here. Yet the road leading to Cheesman is a narrow shelf road, not safe enough for boat-haulers meeting each other on curves. Upgrading the road would cost a fortune, and then there would be the problem of managing boating, policing boaters, limiting their numbers and finding ones that don't return by closing time.

Once again, a concessionaire would be the simplest answer because a limited number of the right boats could be rented from a floating dock that could follow the lake's fluctuations. This would avoid the need to fix the road or to build a long and steep boat ramp—and it would relieve the DWB of management headaches. **Prospective concessionaires may contact Bob Taylor at (303) 628-6000. (Please!)**

For those who fish Cheesman now, the lake offers some good times. "Sometimes, fishing at Cheesman is only fair," says DOW Biologist Jim Satterfield, "but at times it's extraordinary."

Artificial flies and lures only. The special limit for trout is two over 16 inches. Normal limits apply to all other fish. Kokanee snagging is permitted from Sept. 1 through Dec. 31. Ice fishing is banned, and lake fishing closes from Jan. 1 through April 30.

Steelhead planted in the river and in Goose Creek have moved down into the lake to mature. No one can say if this experiment will really work because the mortality rate among steelhead is very high. Only three to five per cent may survive to maturity. Surviving adults might begin their spawning run as early as 1993, but 94 and 95 are more likely. If it works, Goose Creek and the river inlet should provide an exotic angling experience.

Because the shore is so hard to access, both the DWB and the DOW have been building trails.

Shoreline Trail, located to your right as you enter the gate, leads two miles along the bank to the Goose Creek inlet and beyond. It soon forks, the left fork following the shore around the point and the right fork shortcutting over a ridge. At the inlet, the trail crosses the cove on a footbridge, then goes on around the other side of the inlet for a ways.

But that's only a sample of Cheesman's 18 miles of shoreline! It's all technically open to fishing, except for the first mile to your left as you enter the gate, including the spillway and dam. **You must stay off the dam, but may walk any other section of road in the area.**

To avoid the dam, the DOW has built a short but steep trail down below the dam that will take you across the river to access roads along the other side of the lake. Unlike Gill Trail, Cheesman trails are closed in winter (Jan 1-April 30), but fishermen who want to access the river just below the dam are allowed to enter the gate and walk roads to the footbridge.

Beginning at the gate, walk the road straight ahead toward the dam. This mile is the only shore section closed to fishing. Just before you reach the dam, take the road that branches to your left, climbing uphill. Higher up the road forks, but keep to the left. The right fork leads to another caretaker's residence called the Cave Dwellers, which you'll see later. Then the road pitches downhill and ends at a footbridge that crosses the river just below the dam.

Downstream you'll see a bit of trail used by fishermen, but this does not really connect to Gill, as explained. Hardy souls can scramble the route, just as wildlife officers do, but it is dangerous and difficult. It's a nasty place to break a leg.

Upstream you will see a cable marking the no-fishing boundary 1,000 feet below the base of the dam. The switchbacks begin across the bridge, taking you up through timber to a road at the top of the canyon. When you reach the road, notice the Cliff Dwellers cabin perched on the cliffs across canyon. Turn to the left and hike the road until it joins the road coming from the dam. Again turn left and you will be hiking along the east shoreline.

In the fall, many people explore Cheesman just to watch our nation's symbol. Caretaker Ed Christiansen reports seeing as many as 16 bald eagles at a time. Young ones look much like goldens, all brown, but goldens don't fish. Bald eagles attain their white plumage with maturity and they live mostly on fish.

Dogs must be on a leash (strictly enforced). No swimming or wading (no water-body contact at all), no hunting, firearms or fireworks, no fires, no camping, horses or bikes, no ice fishing. Pack your trash. Caretakers vigorously patrol in boats and with trained security dogs to make sure that backpackers don't try to camp along remote shorelines. Remember, you must return to your car within one half hour after sunset.

The only access to the upper reaches of the lake are by four-wheel roads. Perhaps the best is the newly improved (but still four-wheel) Corral Creek road that branches off FS 211 to access the west side of the river miles above the lake. On the east side two others branch off FS #360, which you pick up just south of Westcreek (off 67 between Deckers and Woodland Park). One route goes down toward the Turkey Creek inlet, but a locked gate means that you have to walk from there down the creek to reach the lake. The other route is called Northrup and is a very rough track that actually goes to a ridge above the river well above the reservoir.

STRONTIA SPRINGS RESERVOIR, 98 surface acres, deepest part 206 ft., altitude 6,000 ft., completed 1983.

ROAD DIRECTIONS: Strontia Springs Reservoir can only be reached by trails. The easiest way is Upper Strontia Trail, which begins at the South Platte townsite at the confluence of the North and South Forks of the South Platte River. From Denver, take Highway

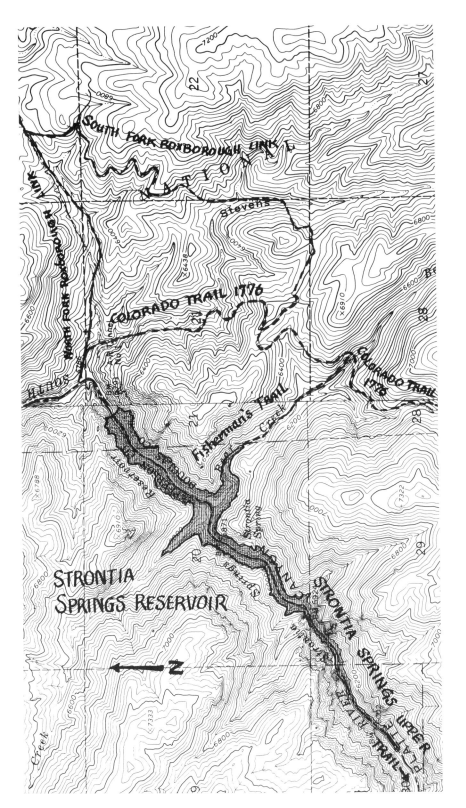

285 south. Just past Conifer, turn left on Foxton Road (County 97). Past Reynolds Park, take a left on County 96 and follow the river downstream to its confluence. The trail begins across the street from the boarded-up South Platte Hotel. From Deckers, go north on Hwy 67, following the river downstream to the confluence. The trail is a locked access road: It is 1.5 miles one-way to the lake.

WATERTON CANYON TRAIL begins at the Waterton Canyon Recreation Area parking lot at Kassler, south of Chatfield Reservoir. From Denver take I-25 South to Colorado 470, then west 12.5 miles to Colorado 126 (Wadsworth). Go south on Wadsworth 4.5 miles to its end just before the entrance to Martin Marietta. Turn left onto a side road and continue 0.3 miles, following signs to Waterton Canyon Recreation Area parking lot. From Colorado Springs, take I-25 North past Castle Rock and take the Hwy. 85 exit to Sedalia. Go 5.8 miles past Sedalia and turn left (west) on Titan Road. After three miles this straight road turns left (south). Another 1.7 miles distant, turn right onto Waterton Road. Follow signs for another 2.4 miles to the parking lot at Waterton Canyon.

This is also the trailhead for the Colorado Trail, so you will begin your trek to Strontia by going up Waterton Canyon for 6 miles on a closed access road, then climb switchbacks on a single track to go up and around the dam. After reaching a high saddle, the Colorado Trail dips to cross the Bear Creek drainage. Distance from parking lot: 8 miles. At that dip, watch for a side trail to your right that follows Bear Creek down to STRONTIA. You will not see the reservoir from the high trail.

If you thought Gross and Cheesman were hard to fish, wait till you see Strontia Springs! Get yourself a mountain bicycle. Strontia is so far from anywhere that a mountain bike will make the long journey over access roads much faster. The upper route is 1.5 miles, but the lower route is over eight miles each way!

This deep lake was made by damming the river's gorge and although it is 1.7 miles long, its banks are so steep (cliffs mostly) that only two small inlets are really accessible. However, the two trails leading to those inlets offer miles of additional fishing along the South Platte. Watch the signs because fishing regs change along sections of the lower river.

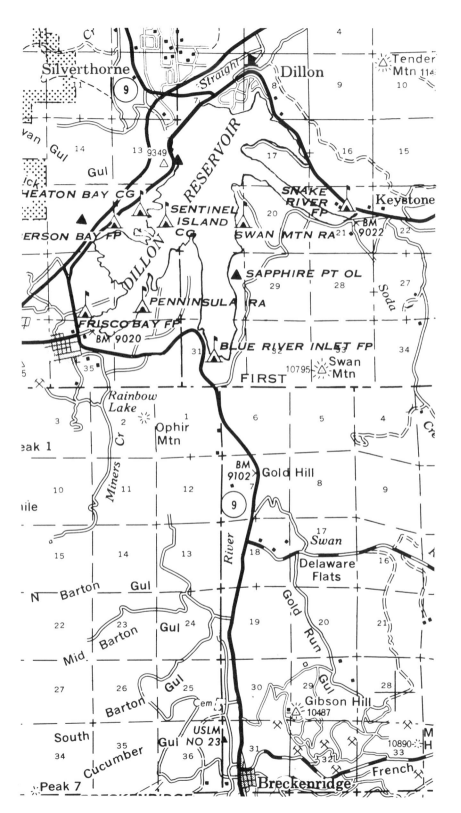

The lake itself is stocked with catchable size rainbow trout, some of which grow to large size. It also has a few browns because the river at each end is famed for browns, as well as rainbow. The lake limit is two fish. Do not attempt to hike around the lake, which is dangerous, or approach the dam, which is off limits. The entire northwest shore is also off limits because this is a special habitat for bighorn sheep.

The best fishing is at Bear Creek inlet, which is also the hardest to reach. No boats, kayaks or floatation devices of any kind are allowed. No dogs are permitted along the lower access, again because of the bighorns, which often come right down to the trails. A dog leash law is strictly enforced along Upper Strontia Trail.

No swimming or fireworks are allowed. Firearms and bows are only permitted during hunting season. You are permitted to camp at the inlets, but its pretty rocky. Ice fishing is permitted.

DILLON RESERVOIR, 3,233 surface acres, deepest point 231 ft., altitude 9,017 ft.,completed in 1963.

ROAD DIRECTIONS: To find DILLON RESERVOIR, drive 70 miles west on I-70 west. It extends south of the highway from Dillon to Frisco at the confluence of the Blue and Snake Rivers and Ten Mile Creek. Good access roads rim the lake.

Though catchable rainbow are still the mainstay, splake and Arctic char may make Dillion one of Colorado's more exotic fishing spots. It is already one of the state's largest and most popular recreation sites.

In the Far North, Arctic char run to the sea and grow to 20 lbs.on the ocean's rich food supply, but this landlocked form won't grow that large at Dillon. "They're doing pretty well," says DOW Biologist Clee Sealing. "They're new to the lake, stocked in the fall of 1990, but they're growing. We're not sure how big they'll get because Dillon is a high lake without as much food. We all hope they eat mysis."

Whatever the Arctic char do, Dillon is definitely becoming a splake lake. A female lake trout and a male brook trout (both types of char) produce this fall-spawning crossbreed that grows faster than lake trout. They don't reproduce, but can reach 14 lbs. in about 10 years, and they have a habit that endears them to anglers: They're hook hungry. If splake don't make it at Dillion, it will be because they all got caught.

In late May of 1992, DOW samplings netted splake in the 14 to 15-inch range, with some reaching 16 inches. Even better, they had high fat content and were stuffed with mysis!

That's great news because Dillon has double trouble: too many suckers and too many mysis, a transparent freshwater shrimp. Mysis were supposed to be trout fodder, but they have the habit of staying away from light, so they stay deep in daylight—where trout can't see them—and they only come up at night—when trout can't see them. Their favorite food is daphnia, or water fleas, that also feed trout, so the double competition from suckers and mysis is starving trout, especially the browns.

Browns caught near shore—and there are very few of them—have practically no body fat and not enough energy for spawning. Only browns caught below 60 feet have body fat because those browns feed on midge. "Browns may be on their way out at Dillon," lamented DOW Biologist Jake Bennett. "Even the rainbow have a hard time carrying over to another season. We only found one rainbow in our May sampling."

Fluctuating levels make Dillon a tough place for trout because shallow areas dry up, so the lake is heavily stocked with catchable rainbows. Bank fishing is best during the early summer months. Dillon's 26.8 miles of shoreline have many access points, and there are boat ramps at Frisco Bay, Frisco Marina, Blue River Inlet and Peak 1 Campground.

Surrounding mountain peaks make this a very scenic lake, but the same peaks make it harder to see bad weather approaching, so sudden winds and boating accidents are not rare, and any spill can be deadly because of the water's cold temperature.

The Forest Service operates seven campgrounds around the lake. For reservations call 1-800-283-2267.

Incidentally, building this lake required relocating the entire town of Dillon, plus 13 miles of highway, 8 miles of transmission lines, a hydroelectric plant and a forest ranger station.

PINEY LAKE, 44 surfaces acres, deepest point perhaps 50 ft., altitude 9,400 ft., natural glacial lake.

ROAD DIRECTIONS: Take I-70 west to the Vail Village Exit. Take the north frontage road (west). Turn right onto Red Sandstone Road and climb the switchbacks past two National Forest campgrounds. You'll see the Piney Lake sign on your left. Distance:13 miles from Vail.

As you walk the little path to Piney Lake, a small valley opens up with high red sandstone cliffs on your left, the Gore Range ahead and a pine ridge on your right. And in the middle is Piney Lake, not a great fishing lake, but a very pretty place.

Vail Associates operates the Piney River Ranch under lease from the DWB and the White River National Forest, but **you can fish there for free.** The road gets heavy drifts, so it and the ranch generally don't open until Memorial Day.

The ranch rents canoes, row boats and fishing equipment and sells bait. They also offer guided horseback rides and sell pack lunches, but you cannot spend the night on the ranch. Indeed, when Vail Associates brings conventioneers up here, they arrive by bus for barbecues and the like.

The lake itself is not currently stocked, but might be in 1993. It may have a few browns and cutthroats, but is mostly populated by small brook trout. The river below in the National Forest is considered much better, but you may only camp in designated campsites such as those you passed on the way up.

Piney might someday be swallowed by a larger reservoir as part of the Eagle-Colorado Collection System.

RALSTON RESERVOIR, 182 surface acres, deepest part 131 ft. altitude 6,046 ft., completed in 1937.

ROAD DIRECTIONS: To find RALSTON RESERVOIR and LONG LAKES, take Colo. Hwy 72 northwest to Colo. 93 (Foothills Road), then go three miles south on Foothills Road to the reservoir access turnoff on your right. From Golden take Foothills Road approximately 6 miles to the access road.

Nobody has asked to open Ralston Reservoir. It has been drained twice in two years, has no fish and the DOW didn't find any when they drained it the first time. Back when its levels were more stable, Ralston was supposed to have some sizable rainbows that originated in Ralston Creek, but it fluctuates more now and has other problems. Its banks are the steepest of any DWB lake (with the possible exception of Strontia Springs) and they're made of dirt that sluffs away into the water even when nobody is clawing and tromping around the shore. Trailbuilding at Ralston would be challenging, to say the least, and very expensive.

"What we'd rather see at Ralston is a place for schools to bring groups to study the unique shortgrass prairie environment at Ralston and the riparian environment below," said Bob Taylor, DWB environmental coordinator.

The really nice fishing is closeby at Long Lakes.

LONG LAKES (2 of them), 5 to 15 surface acres, deepest point about 15 ft., altitude 6,000 ft., upper completed in 1873, lower in 1909.

These beautiful prairie lakes are much better fisheries than Ralston. They are already full of largemouth bass and yellow perch and have plenty of minnows and crayfish in the shallows. As Bob Taylor and I walked up, we could see largemouth bass spawning in the shallows. One big female had to be at least three pounds. It might be a good place to stock walleye, too.

Both lakes are on a grassy hillside southeast of Ralston. What looks like a mine tunnel on the west side of the upper reservoir is actually an inlet tunnel carrying water from Ralston. The hillside below it is marked with green streaks and creases where the water from the upper lake seeps below ground to the lower one. If it weren't for their concrete valve works, you'd never know they were reservoirs. They look like large farm ponds.

We saw ducks, geese and a herd of mule deer in the area where work is being done to widen a ditchwork into a string of tiny ponds. The DWB is also digging around the base of a hill

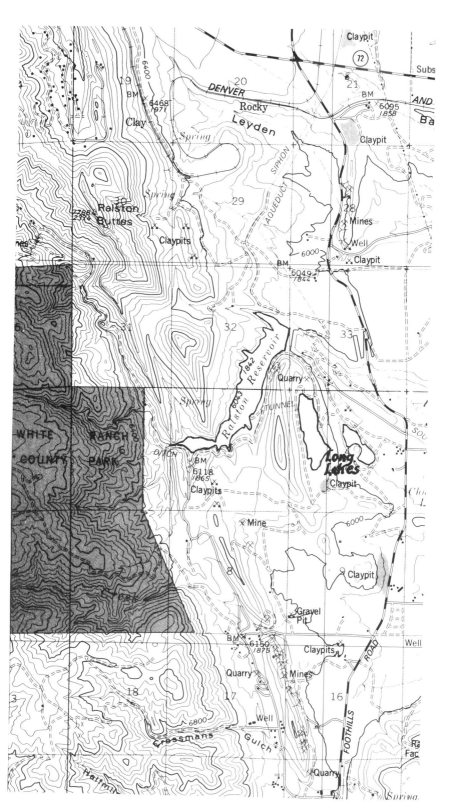

beside the lower lake to create an island where ducks may be able to nest without as much pressure from ground predators.

The present access road comes right from the Ralston operations center, so the DWB would like to create a new access from above in order to avoid the center. An agreement with Western Paving might create the right-of-way.

Compared to other closed waters in the Denver Water Board system, Long Lakes seem to have fewer problems and a brighter future, but they will need recreation management.

MARSTON RESERVOIR, 635 surface acres, deepest part40 ft., altitude 5,503 ft., completed in 1902..

ROAD DIRECTIONS: To find MARSTON from Denver, take Santa Fe Dr. south to Hampden Ave, then west on Hampden to Sheridan Boulevard and south on Sheridan to Quincy Ave. Go west on Quincy for about half a mile. The reservoir is next to the Marston Treatment Plant at 6100 West Quincy, about three miles northwest of Littleton. From Colorado Springs, take I-25 north to west Hampden, then repeat above.

Marston has received a lot of hopeful publicity because it is chuck full of nice walleye. Not that walleye breed there, mind you. They have to be stocked, but in turn they supply milt for hatcheries to rear walleye for stocking other waters— and for restocking Marston itself.

You might think the Division of Wildlife would be reluctant to open such an important resource, but not so. They feel Marston could stand some legal harvest because there are plenty of good fish, and sneak-ins are already cutting the fence to fish the lake (and are even pulling up the DOW's nets to get at the fish).

With three holes in the chain link fence when we visited, you might also think the local neighborhood would be hot to open Marston, but again, not so. Fashionable Bow Mar residents keep the water board's phones busy with protests and complaints about the push to open Marston.

Imagine a lake held captive within a steep wall of rip-rap with a road on top of the wall all the way around. A chain-link fence

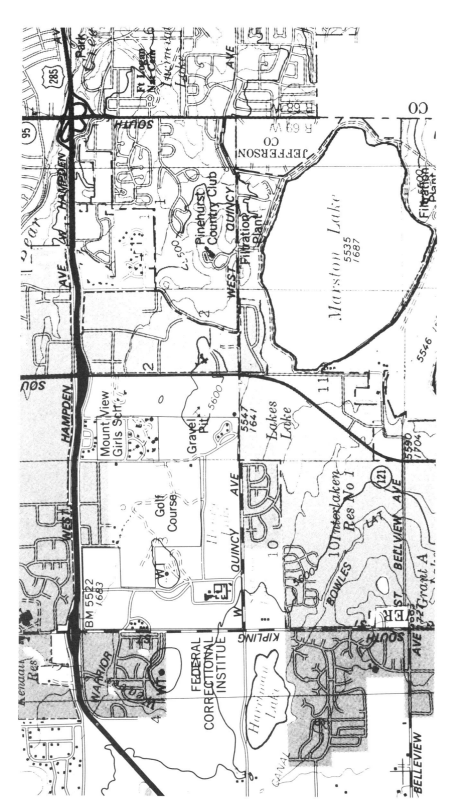

separates the walled-in reservoir from apartment projects and high-dollar homes. When the lake is unusually high. it would be a lot of trouble for bank anglers to scramble around on that rip-rap, which shifts underfoot, but that's not the real problem because Marston is rarely that full. Generally, the water doesn't get near the rip-rap except at a couple of points.

Most of the time, Marston is an oval lake surrounded by a wide and soft mud flat. You can't wade it because the mud is too soft. In fact, there are only two small places at the narrow ends of the oval where bank fishermen could reach the water. That's at the river inlet and at the opposite end near the treatment plant itself. Most of the shoreline is only available to birds!

That's why both the DWB and the DOW want boats on Marston. When the DOW works the lake, they do it in a boat and that would be the only way for more than a few fishermen to keep out of the mud.

Which brings up some other problems: how to limit the numbers of anglers, where to put parking, how to choose an access route against neighborhood opposition. And who would manage the recreation here?

The simplest solution would be for a concessionaire to come in and run the place, renting a fleet of boats from a floating dock that could follow the lake's fluctuations. Prospective concessionaires can contact Bob Taylor at the water department at (303) 628-6000.

With both the Denver Water Board and the Division of Wildlife agreeing that Marston should open, something may work out. But the walleye are certainly ready, as well as a thriving population of yellow perch and some big trout, too.

HARRIMAN RESERVOIR, 59 surface acres, deepest part 13 ft., altitude 5,500 ft., completed 1873.

ROAD DIRECTIONS: HARRIMAN RESERVOIR located on West Quincy Avenue just southwest of its intersection with Kipling. Do not confuse it with the private lake immediately southeast of that intersection. For directions to West Quincy, see Marston.

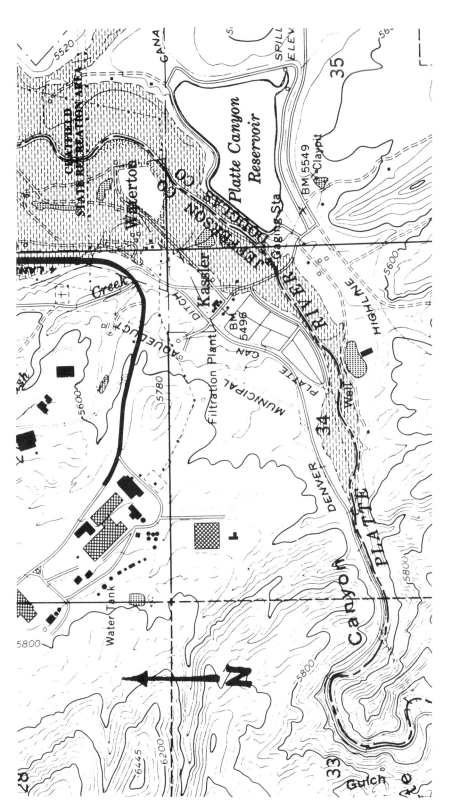

Many years ago, Harriman was a largemouth bass and crappie fishery open to the public through an arrangement with the DOW and the Isaac Walton League, but it was closed because it was trashed out and vandalized, according to Bob Taylor, environmental coordinator for the DWB.

Now the DWB is ready to try again, perhaps this time with management by a local recreation district.

Harriman looks like a beautiful urban park lake with gentle grassy banks and some large trees set back from the shore, but the murky water is a sign that carp have taken over and those will have to be dealt with before it can be restored and restocked. DOW Biologists Jim Satterfield believes the rough fish will have to be killed out with retenone.

"Carp act like vacuum cleaners on the bottom, stirring up mud," Satterfield explained. "I've seen a lake clear up overnight when the carp are taken out."

If the recreation district agrees to manage Harriman, this may be the next Denver Water Board lake to open.

PLATTE CANYON RESERVOIR, 58 surface acres, deepest part 38 ft., elevation 5,534 ft., completed 1904.

ROAD DIRECTIONS: From Denver take I-25 South to Colorado 470, then west 12.5 miles to Colorado 126 (Wadsworth). Go south on Wadsworth 4.5 miles to its end just before the entrance to Martin Marietta. Turn left onto a side road marked for Roxborough State Park. The reservoir will be on your left less a quarter of a mile farther.

From Colorado Springs, take I-25 North past Castle Rock and take the Hwy. 85 exit to Sedalia. Go 5.8 miles past Sedalia and turn left (west) on Titan Road. After three miles this straight road turns left (south). Another 1.7 miles distant, turn right onto Waterton Road. The reservoir will be on your right just before reaching the Kassler Treatment Plant.

Visitors exploring the High Like Canal peer through a high chain-link fence at a lake where ducks and geese swim. This is Platte Canyon Reservoir, settling pond for the Kassler

Treatment Plant, but since that plant is closing, the time may be right to take down the fence and open this grassy-banked lake to recreation.

Access is no problem here, and there is room to build a parking lot, so the only obstacle seems to be the question of management. Only 25 miles south-southwest of Denver, this site will need some enforcement to keep it from becoming a night party spot, but the DWB is exploring options.

Recently drained to repair the dam, the lake probably has very few fish right now. But as we explored it, schools of minnows broke the surface and large frogs leaped from the reeds. All in all, it looks like the kind of habitat that could be managed for walleye, bass, crappie and perch.

The dam is rip-rap, but the rest of the lake is surrounded by near-level grass. "This will be open and it will be neat," Bob Taylor told us. "But it may be a ways down the road."

AURORA LAKES
5 Open to All
1 Closed.(But Has No Fish)

Quincy Reservoir (Open)
Aurora Reservoir (Open)
Spinney Reservoir (Open)
Jefferson Lake (Open)
Homestake Reservoir (Open, See Colo. Spgs.)
Rampart Reservoir (Closed, But No Fish)

Aurora could be Colorado's model city for modern water and recreation management. Aurora has benefited in every way by opening every drinking water reservoir with any recreational potential, even its terminal reservoirs. For environmental reasons, it turns out that good water and good fishing go together.

"When you have a lake that you leave alone without the full ecological cycle, you soon find out why natural systems are so important," says Pete Smith, Manager of Water Operations. **"You need the full life cycle, including healthy fish, to have good water quality."**

Smith explained that Quincy Reservoir, a terminal reservoir, used to have quality problems when closed to fishing. Water fleas were plugging up filters. So the Division of Wildlife began working to establish a natural ecosystem. They added various types of fish, starting with Mississippi silversides, a type of minnow. Now the lake has everything from crayfish to help control weed growth to giant, non-reproducing tiger muskie to control other fish. **The result is cleaner water that is also trophy fishing water, the kind of lake where records are shattered over and over again.**

Best of all, Aurora's ambitious recreational program is designed to more or less pay for itself. The public is obviously willing to pay user fees and rental fees. When the city began renting canoes and boats with quiet electric motors at Quincy in 1988, **rentals paid for their capital expenditures within the first three months!**

And when the city opened Aurora Reservoir in 1991, 5,000 people lined up to buy passes and rent boats. Again, the boat rental program paid for itself within the first season! The city's Park and Recreation Dept. is obviously thriving as much as the fish are.

In the mountains, the Colorado Department of Parks and Outdoor Recreation operates Aurora's Spinney Reservoir, a Gold Medal favorite with trout fishermen. Aurora's Jefferson Lake near Kenosha Pass has been jammed with anglers for years. Aurora shares water rights at Homestake, also open (see Colorado Springs), and the only lake it has closed is a muddy impoundment called Rampart Reservoir (not to be confused with the Colorado Springs lake of the same name).

"We've never had any pressure or request to open Rampart because it just doesn't have any fishing potential," Smith explained. "It's banks are messy and muddy. It's water level fluctuates so wildly that it breaks the food chain in those vital nearshore areas. It's just a wide place in the aqueduct really."

Rampart is located southeast of Strontia Springs Reservoir and won't merit more discussion here. We call it "closed" because you need a key to get in.

Indeed, Quincy and Aurora Reservoirs may look odd in a book that is mostly about mountain lakes (it will take another book to describe the thousands of acres of closed public waters at lower elevations). But **Quincy and Aurora Reservoirs serve as examples of how reservoirs—even terminal reservoirs—can be opened—even to boating—at no great expense or danger to a city.**

Someone once joked that a terminal reservoir is defined as a lake that water managers would rather die than open. Actually, a terminal reservoir is the final lake in a chain, the last settling pond before treatment. Opening such lakes to fishing is either possible or impossible, depending on who you talk to. Aurora's experience shows that fishing these sensitive areas is perhaps better than leaving them alone.

After hearing so much about Quincy's boating program, we were shocked to see how simple it was. The so-called boat ramp at Quincy is nothing expensive, just a tiny narrow beach made of pebbles the size of your thumb. When we first arrived, there was no ranger around, so people were filling out their own passes and stuffing money-filled envelopes into a slot. Locals with permits were carrying their own boats to the water without any baby-sitting. The ranger soon showed up to fill out permits for new-comers and break out the electric motors and batteries for rentals, but **it was obviously a simple and convenient and inexpensive system that anglers enjoy.**

Which made us wonder why other communities fret so much about the imagined expense and complication of boating on less-sensitive, non-terminal reservoirs.

ROAD DIRECTIONS: QUINCY and AURORA RESERVOIRS are both located on Quincy Avenue east of Cherry Creek Reservoir south-east of Denver. Take Parker Road (also called Hwy. 83 from Colorado Springs) to Quincy Avenue and head east. The first gate is 2.4 miles from that intersection. The main entrance with boat ramp is half a mile farther. The turnoff to AURORA RESERVOIR is another five miles east. The way is well marked.

QUINCY RESERVOIR, 155 surface acres, deepest point 54 ft., built in 1973, opened to fishing 1983, opened to boating 1988.

Once an artificial impoundment with a water flea problem, Quincy has been reborn as a trophy fishery.

"It's probably the best tiger muskie fishery in the state," says DOW Biologist Jim Satterfield. And here's the proof: The current state record for tiger muskie is a 45.75-inch monster weighing 27 pounds and 3 ounces caught by Richard A. Allen at Quincy, but the previous record was also set at Quincy for a 21-pound 12-ounce muskie caught the very same day! Indeed, 14 of the 18 state tiger muskie records have been set at Quincy. And since muskies are new, no one yet knows how big they might get.

Look at the snapshots in the ranger's shack of proud anglers, holding up their catches. Look at that 26-inch rainbow, the 23-

inch brown, the 15-inch yellow perch. Large mouth bass run to 6.5 pounds and the average trout runs between 13 and 16 inches.

"**We like to encourage catch-and-release,**" says Ranger Milton Hunholz. "You can take home two trout over 16 inches, but about one trout in seven is 16 inches, so your chances are good."

Unlike Aurora, Quincy is a sport fishing lake with rustic services, not a place for a family picnic. Indeed, food consumption is banned, but 3.2 beer is allowed. People sometimes stroll around the lake (4.5 miles) to watch blue heron or red fox, but bicycling is banned. You must stay off the spillway, so you have to walk the road to complete the circle. **Fishing is by flies and artificial lures only.**

Quincy is an urban lake surrounded by housing on three sides. Unlike nearby Cherry Creek, the water is very clear. Cottonwoods line the shore.

A day pass is required, $3 each for ages 7-61, $22 for a season pass. Senior citizens pay $2 each, ages 62 and over, $18 for a season pass. There is also a Quincy-Aurora combination pass that saves you money. Quincy is open March 1 to Nov. 30, depending on ice. Hour are dawn to dusk, except for one day a month (either a Friday or Saturday) when full moon fishing runs to 11 p.m.

You can rent a 17-foot canoe or 12-foot row boat with electric motor for $9 an hour with a two-hour minimum, cash only. All boats must stay 150 feet away from occupied shoreline, avoid buoyed areas and leave the water by half an our after sundown.

Or you can bring your own boat and pay a $4 daily fee. The season permit is $35 for residents and $40 for non-residents. No gasoline motors are allowed, except for the ranger, and no sailcraft are allowed because the lake is so small. But since trailers are not allowed in the water, you have to bring a boat that you can hand-carry to the water. Tubes with waders are also allowed.

A dock near the boat ramp is provided mainly for handicapped anglers. That doesn't mean that non-handicapped folks can't use it, but when handicapped anglers show up, please be considerate. A wheelchair accessible portable restroom is provided.

Rules: No pets, **no bait fishing**, no firearms, no camping, no swimming or water-body contact, no bicycles, no fires, no food consumption, no littering, no glass containers, no alcohol except for 3.2. Don't disturb or take away vegetation or wildlife. You may fish with waders, but watch out for drop-offs! The ranger has a map with underwater topography, but it can't show every hole. Christmas trees have been placed in the lake to improve habitat.

The daily bag and possession limits are two trout 16 inches and over, six bass 15 inches and over and one tiger muskie over 20 inches. State limits apply to other fish. Have fun!

AURORA RESERVOIR, 805 surface acres, deepest point 110 ft., built in 1989, opened in 1991.

Family recreation was part of the plan for Aurora Reservoir all along. Elaborate facilities are still being built, but Aurora is already popular as a place where families picnic, barbecue, swim and sun at the beach, sail and scuba dive, bicycle and boat and wind surf. The 8.5-mile bike path circling the lake is paved and smooth enough for a baby stroller. You can take your dog, so long as it remains on a leash and stays well away from the beach.

Filling a basin on the high plains, this lake has the bluest and clearest water you can imagine. A glassful dipped from the center looks like tapwater because it already meets clarity standards (but they do filter it anyway). Do your part by treading lightly on the prairie grass and use the bike path whenever possible.

A few large brood fish have been released here, but most of its fish are as young as the lake itself. **This water will support both cold and warm-water species, so it is being heavily stocked with fry. For example, three and half million walleye in 1990, 200,000 in '91, and another million in '92. Rainbow, wiper, largemouth bass, channel catfish, crappie and yellow perch are also being stocked. Bait fishing is permitted.**

"Next year (93) we should see an explosion of walleye," says Ranger Rick Mueller, "and the warm water species should really bloom in '94."

After surveying the lake in April of 1992, DOW Biologist Jim Satterfield agreed. "We found a fantastic trout population, considering this lake was bone dry only three years ago. The wipers are already 12 and 13 inches long, and the yellow perch are doing well. In fact, everything is going right at Aurora. It's hot!"

You may fish anywhere except the sand beaches, even from the dam. The limit is two trout of any size, four largemouth bass 15 inches or longer, four Walleye 15 inches and over, four wiper 14 inches and over. State limits apply to all others.

There are two beaches, one for swimming and one for wind surfing. You may swim only in designated areas. Yes, your body can touch this terminal drinking water, but the lake is large and is being closely monitored. There is no water skiing because only the authorities can use gasoline-powered boats. All others use electric, wind or muscle. If you bring a gasoline motor, it must remain in the raised position and all portable gas tanks must be removed from the boat.

Aurora has the same successful canoe and boat rental program as Quincy, but you can also rent sailboards here. This larger lake is also popular with people who own sailboats. A new marina is underway and boaters will be able to rent moorings and drydock storage. A city park is under construction nearby, which will include overnight camping facilities. A golf course is being constructed to the west, and to the northwest is a horse racetrack.

Bring a hat and sunscreen. Trees are being planted, but it will be a few years before they provide much shade. Shelters are also being constructed, along with a concession stand and general store.

A day pass is required, but it is $3 per car instead of per person, $25 for a resident season pass, $30 for non resident. Other rules: No glass containers, no littering, no firearms, no alcohol except 3.2%. Aurora is open all year round, dawn to dusk.

SPINNEY MOUNTAIN RESERVOIR, 2,400 surface acres, deepest point 60 ft., built in 1981.

ROAD DIRECTIONS: SPINNEY is located five miles upstream from ELEVENMILE in South Park. The most scenic route from Denver is Hwy 285 to Fairplay. SPINNEY is 23 miles south of Fairplay via Hwy 9. Turn left where 9 T-junctions at Hwy 24. The way is well marked from Hartsel. From Colorado Springs, take Hwy. 24 west past Lake

George and over Wilkerson pass. Then turn left onto a well-marked dirt road where there are remnants of an old cabin. Follow signs.

Spinney Mountain is one of only two Gold Medal fishing lakes in Colorado, and the streams both above and below are Gold Medal water, too, so this is definitely trophy country! The river is catch-and-release only, but **at Spinney, you can keep one trout at least 20 inches long.** This actually means that much of your fun at Spinney will amount to catch-and-release also. Still, the richness of the habitat means that you'll be angling for good-sized fish, even if you don't wind up with a keeper.

When Spinney first opened, the DOW was horrified at how many anglers wanted to take home a full stringer of eight huge trout, so the special limit is designed to protect the resource. But Gold Medal designation means there are plenty left and thriving. Fishing is by **artificial flies and lures only.**

When this lake thaws and opens around the end of April, about 2,000 fishermen generally show up for the opening. Fishing is permitted from one half hour before sunup to one half hour after sundown. The lake generally closes around the end of October, depending upon ice. **Ice fishing is banned.**

Located in the high prairie of South Park with distant mountains all around, **Spinney can be a very windy place, so boaters need to be especially careful. Boats have overturned and drownings have occurred.**

There are two access points. The best boat ramp is on the southern arm, but this one is not usable when the lake is low later in the summer. If you have to use the old one on the north side, try to borrow somebody else's boat. The north ramp has sharp, square-cornered blocks on the ends of the ties, so if you don't back your trailer straight, they can snag a tire. The ramp is also highly exposed, so if you have to come in under windy conditions (generally a westerly crosswind) murky waves will make those blocks hard to see and can puncture the boat.

Still, you can do well fishing from the bank at Spinney because cutthroat come in close. A good spot is on the dam's rip rap or the dam's north corner where the dam meets the mountain. The cove on the south side is hot in the spring just after ice-out.

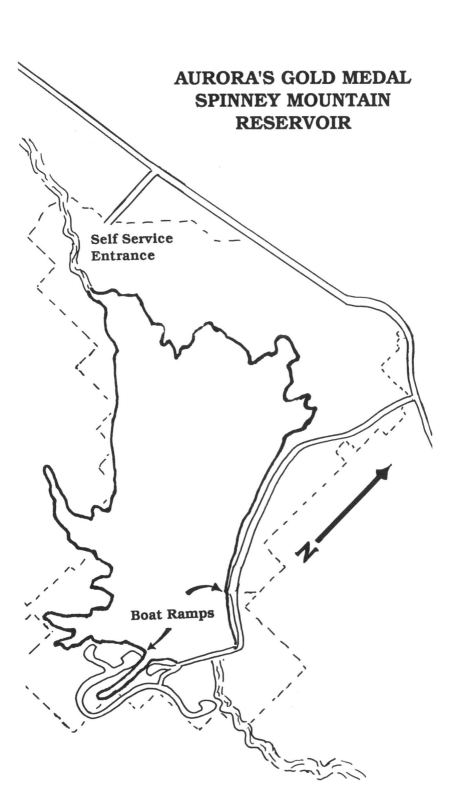

AURORA'S GOLD MEDAL
SPINNEY MOUNTAIN
RESERVOIR

**Self Service
Entrance**

Boat Ramps

N

Chest waders allow you to access a lot of water because of the lake's gently sloping bottom. It is also popular with belly-boaters.

This lake is designed to capture runoff, so it starts low and fills through June, then gradually goes down through the rest of the season. The best fishing is right after ice-off (before fish get re-educated). Both Snake River cutthroats and rainbows are being stocked in the 10-inch size, plus additional cuts in the 7-inch size.

The DOW tried to remove the northern pike when this lake was built, but they sneaked back in via the stream above, probably from ranch ponds upstream. Unlike nearby Elevenmile, however, there are no great numbers of small pike to snap off your trout gear and the large pike control the population by eating their own kind. Thus, you have a much better chance of catching a trophy pike over 30 inches at Spinney.

Fishing a homemade orange egg-pattern fly—standard at Spinney early in the season—Gary Morse of Colorado Springs thought he had hooked into a big cutthroat while belly boating here in 1991. Morse had only a three-pound-test leader on his nine-foot flyrod, so he had to fin desperately to follow the fish in and out of weeds for 45 minutes, while a crowd of onlookers gathered on shore. It turned out to be a 39.25-inch northern, 13 pounds and 13 ounces, big but not exceptional for South Park. Yet when Morse checked the National Freshwater Hall of Fame records, it turned out to be a line-class record for such light tackle.

"It was hooked right at the edge of the mouth, "Morse told the Gazette Telegraph. "That was every fortunate—otherwise its teeth would probably have shredded the leader."

The state record for kokanee salmon was also set at Spinney (six pounds, three ounces, 27.5 inches), but that was a fluke. It probably swam down from Antero. Salmon are not stocked at Spinney.

Eighteen miles of great river fishing should be added upstream soon. Badger Basin Ranch will add 10 miles to your South Fork fishing and another eight miles along the Middle Fork. The legislature has okayed the deal and the DOW is now acquiring the rights. Watch the news for word of the opening.

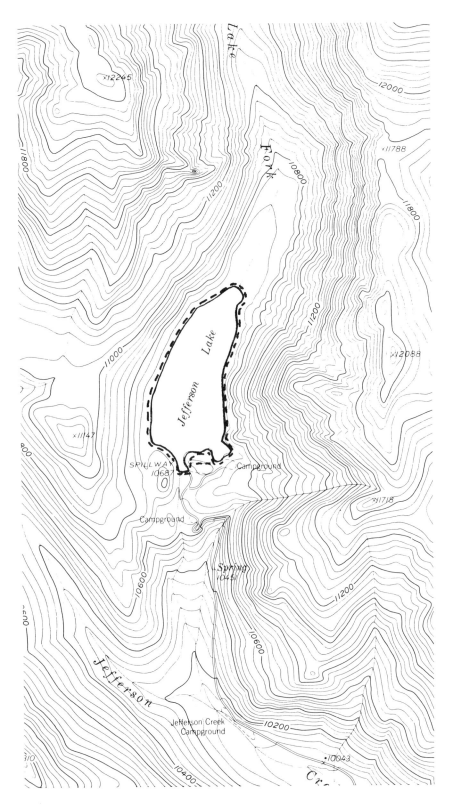

JEFFERSON LAKE, 115 surface acres, deepest point 175 ft.; altitude 10,687 ft.,natural lake, but dam was built in 1889.

ROAD DIRECTIONS: JEFFERSON LAKE is west of Grant in Park County. The turnoff is at Jefferson on Hwy. 285 south of Kenosha Pass. The way is well marked and the road is good. Distance: 8 miles. On the way, you'll pass Lodgepole and Jefferson Campgrounds. There is no camping at the lake itself.

High mountain scenery and lots of recreation make Jefferson Lake one of the most popular destinations in Park County. Unlike Spinney, Jefferson is a postcard forest lake open all year round.

Ice fishing and cross-country skiing lure visitors in the winter, and when the lake thaws in late May, two nearby campgrounds fill up with families who come to fish and boat, picnic, hike and mountain bike. No camping is allowed at the lake itself, but you'll pass Lodgepole and Jefferson Campgrounds on the way. To make a reservation call 1-800-283-2267. These are pay campgrounds, but additional free parking for day-users is located just outside of the Jefferson Campground.

Jefferson is now stocked chiefly with 10-inch rainbow (35,000 a season), some grayling and with kokanee salmon. High altitude results in salmon that are a little smaller. A female that may grow to 20 inches at Elevenmile may reach only 14 inches at Jefferson.

Lakers are no longer stocked at Jefferson, but seem to be reproducing on their own. A special limit of one laker over 20 inches is strictly enforced because some anglers may be harming reproduction by taking smaller ones, perhaps confusing them with other trout. Watch for the deeply notched tail fin that characterizes the laker. You won't catch many over 16 inches, however.

Jefferson has a good boat ramp and bank fishermen will enjoy the 1.5-mile shoreline trail that circles the lake. The trail is best on the eastern side and makes a nice stroll for people who don't ordinarily hike. It's very scenic, but take it easy: The elevation is 10,680 ft.

All in all, there are good reasons why Jefferson is so popular. Just know that it is not a place to "get away from it all."

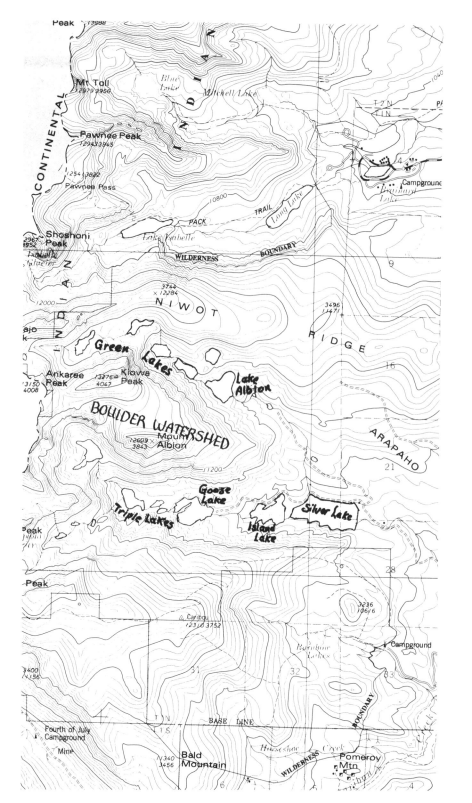

CITY OF BOULDER LAKES
3 Open to All
14 Still Closed to All

Silver Lake (Closed)
Island Lake (Closed)
Goose Lake (Closed)
Lake Albion (Closed)
Green Lakes and Unnamed Lakes (All Closed)
Boulder Reservoir (Open)
Barker Reservoir (Open)
Skyscraper Reservoir (Open)

When backpackers hike along the popular Arapaho Glacier Trail, a high ridge trail in the Indian Peaks Wilderness, they discover a tempting view to the north: An evergreen valley graced with granite formations and sparkling lakes lies practically at their feet.

There is no fence to keep wanderers from drifting downhill toward this scenic wonderland, but there are supposed to be plenty of "No Trespassing" signs (if they haven't been vandalized), warning them not to try it. For if they do, they run right into the full-time caretaker and a vigilant crew of eight young patrol personnel carrying binoculars and walkie-talkies, ready to smack the hand that reaches for forbidden fruit.

Seriously, these kids aren't kidding. Their main job is reported to be maintenance, but they are eager and athletic and very effective watchdogs, beginning their patrols before dawn. They will spot you and report you, generally before you can reach the trees. Then the caretaker may write you a very serious ticket.

This is Boulder's closed watershed—or just a part of it—an

8,000-acre treasure where 14 or so lakes and ponds lay strung along a Y-shaped valley. **This is the most secret and highly guarded of any Colorado watershed, for it is the only watershed guarded by so many personnel and one watershed where we were absolutely denied any official entry,** despite numerous applications in writing and by phone, despite credentials and friendly assurances, despite downright begging and pleading.

The land is wholly owned by the city, and no citizen of another city has any vote, but Boulder residents do enjoy fishing other communities' reservoirs! The city reminded us that Boulder need not be included in this book, but secrecy quite frankly heightened our curiosity and convinced us that Boulder citizens probably have no idea what they really own—and can't enjoy or even visit.

The City of Boulder's written statement was very brief: "This area remains closed primarily due to concerns about water quality, research, threatened & endangered species and nature preserve. We derive approximately 25% of our water (on an annual basis) from this watershed area," signed Robert E. Williams, Assistant Director of Public Works for Utilities.

(This sounds very much like the position taken by Colorado Springs only a few years ago.)

Without official cooperation, our statistics are skimpy, but we flew the area, interviewed the Division of Wildlife, talked to personnel who used to work in the area, indeed anyone who had knowledge of this forbidden land.

What we discovered surprised us—and may surprise you.

Boulder has created the Biafra of the fish world, a place where common brook trout are so overcrowded and starving that they grow pitifully stunted with large heads and small withered bodies. Far from being a completely natural, untouched nature preserve, Boulder is preserving a very unnatural situation where native cutthroats are being crowded out by a growing over-population of alien fish.

Boulder's stated intention is to protect Colorado's original native trout, the threatened Type A greenback. Yet Boulder's cutts are presently classified as Type B, genetically suspect, because of an old report that rainbows were unexplainably introduced into

58

these waters years ago. New DNA tests will begin this summer, which may solve the question of genetic purity.

Yet cutthroats—whatever they are—need special conditions for breeding. Too often, they cannot breed in Colorado lakes because spring runoff makes the inlets too muddy, and when the water clears, too often the flow stops altogether so that inlets dry up before reproduction can be completed. This keeps their numbers down. Add to that a few predators—eagles, otters, even Indian fishermen—and it's easy to see how cutthroats never ate themselves out of house and home in their original natural system.

Brook trout, on the other hand, are alien invaders. Introduced in the past century, they have driven native cutthroats almost to extinction by out-breeding and out-competing them. Brookies can breed almost anywhere and certainly do. By spawning in the fall, they incubate their eggs all winter and emerge a full month ahead of cutthroats. Brookies depend upon heavy predation to keep their numbers down. Otherwise, they can overpopulate their environment and starve each other cruelly until none of them can achieve healthy size. (When not crowded, brookies can grow pretty big. The state record is seven pounds and 10 ounces!)

Without enough predators to control brookie numbers, the scientific remedy for over-population is called fishing. The state encourages fishing for brookies because the harder you fish 'em, the better they do. In fact, the state offers a special brookie bonus. You can take the usual eight brookies over eight inches long, plus an additional 10 brookies eight inches or less. It takes quite a few little ones to make a big meal, but they are renowned as one of the most flavorful of all trout. Eat enough, and the rest will grow to impressive sizes, often 15 inches or more.

So why doesn't the DOW do the humanitarian thing and rescue these fish to release elsewhere? Well, they do. In the past five years, the division has rescued many thousands of brookies from a single lake, Island Lake. They concentrate on one lake because taking a few from many lakes would do no good. Yet the DOW can't use very many. Brookies are so common and prolific that few waters can take more, so there is simply no way the DOW can use enough to put a dent in the Boulder watershed's total problem.

Only anglers could do that.

As for the greenbacks, it is safe to say that many Boulder citizens assume that rare greenbacks thrive protected in most of its forbidden lakes. Not so.

Only one lake, Goose Lake, has cutthroats and no brookies. It's sisters in the southern chain are either fishless from winter kill or share their food with multiplying brookies. Indeed, the lakes of the northern chain, including Lake Albion and the Green Lakes, are entirely populated by stunted brookies.

No mistake, this watershed is considered a marvelous habitat, a rich producer. It's major problem is being overly ready for fishing, so stuffed that it is more than ready to go just as it is. No fish management will be necessary to prepare these waters for sport fishing. On the contrary, sport fishing is the one thing really necessary for fish management here.

Obviously, Boulder's Utility Dept. doesn't want to operate a recreational park, fearing the expense and bother of hiring a game warden, but Boulder anglers we interviewed wondered how that would compare to the expense and bother of hiring so many guards to keep people out! This kind of closure is not cheap.

Almost everyone we interviewed spontaneously mentioned one special quality that may explain why only essential personnel are allowed to see this area. It is incredibly, uniquely beautiful. A number of people offered the comment that it was the most beautiful place they had ever seen. That is very tall praise from folks who know Colorado! If National Geographic ever did a layout, the world would want to come.

Obviously, we can't let the world come all at once. A lot of us want to have our cake and eat it, too, wanting both access and preservation. But the right access, properly done, should also preserve. That is the goal of every true environmentalist.

For one, I can hardly wait. I can't help looking forward to some future day when I might see and fish an area that front-range anglers talk so much about. Being told I cannot even look makes me want to all the more.

Forbidden fruit.

The DOW is not currently pushing to open this area. They enjoy a very good working relationship with Boulder and know that Boulder is not ready to consider such a request. Yet the DOW would honestly jump at the chance. To them it would be the glory of the Rockies, the achievement of a lifetime to open this special place to some kind of highly-regulated, walk-in, low-impact fishing that would both preserve and improve such a unique jewel.

Even the fish need it.

Most of these lakes are natural, some are semi-natural and a few sport regular, unnatural concrete dams and man-made water-falls of 10 feet or so. Thus, it works out that fish from Silver Lake can't possibly reach Island Lake upstream and Island's fish can't possibly reach Goose Lake. Unnatural but handy.

When the DOW nets fish in these lakes, they're taking milt and eggs to be reared in hatcheries for transplant in other regions. They have several such sources and haven't used Boulder's in several years, but may start again soon. Yet while doing so, they note the kinds and sizes of the fish they net.

In Silver Lake, the first and biggest lake, one with a concrete dam, they find cutthroat in the 12 and 14-inch size and brook trout in the 10 to 12-inch range. Cutthroat naturally reproduce in Silver's inlet, but are in some danger from competing brookies.

In Island Lake (which has four islands), they find cutthroats measuring 11 to 14 inches and smaller brookies measuring 10 inches. **Cutthroats naturally reproduce in Island's inlet, but are in great danger of being crowded out by the stunted brook trout. Cutthroats used to be in the majority in Island Lake, but now stunted brookies outnumber the cutthroat and are taking over the lake, despite salvage efforts that have removed thousands.**

In the third major lake, Goose Lake, they find only greenback cutthroats, but in larger sizes (because the dear damned brookies aren't competing). They find a lot of 13 to 15-inch cutts and some up to five pounds! Unlike Pikes Peak's hatchery lakes, Goose Lake sustains its own population without restocking.

The lakes upstream from Goose are shallow and winter kill.

In the northern chain, lakes are deeper and don't winterkill. **All have brookies instead of cutts and Lake Albion's brookies only reach eight or nine inches, no matter how old they get.**

They're all stunted, Boulder's Biafra. The whole chain is that way and probably can't get any more healthy until fishing is allowed.

More intensive sampling will begin in the summer of 1992 and samplings are planned to continue yearly because of the danger to the cutthroats. Colorado's greenbacks will remain on the threatened species list until 20 self-sustaining habitats can be established. Anglers are already permitted to fish for them on a catch-and-release basis in several Colorado lakes, including the Army's Lytle Pond on Fort Carson.

Two years ago the Alpine Club asked Boulder City Council to open its watershed, but the Council unanimously voted it down. According to City Attorney Joseph N. deRaismes III, the city feels that the nearby Indian Peaks Wilderness is theoretically protected, but is still being trashed by over-use, so Boulder hopes to preserve one area as untouched for the benefit of wildlife and study by the Institute for Arctic and Alpine Research.

Trouble is, untouched can also mean neglected. Untouched can mean allowing brook trout to drive out a threatened native species. Untouched can mean letting dead wood build up to create a firetrap. Untouched has led to trouble in other watersheds, as you'll see in the rest of this book.

Can such a unique beauty spot be enjoyed somehow without ruining it?

It has been suggested that a very restrictive system might be established whereby a limited number of people would help with resource management and thereby earn the right to enjoy a unique, highly supervised recreational experience. An environmental course might be required as a qualification, so that applicants would learn about tundra, flora and fauna, identification of species, fire protection and so forth. A lottery might be necessary if too many people qualify. Applicants would then pay a fee to go as a group to the watershed by bus, where their recreation would be supervised. Fishing might be limited to fly and lure only, with greenbacks being released alive and brook trout being harvested. The emphasis would be on low impact: no fires, pack out what you pack in and so forth. Such a system could support itself financially and could be limited to just a few days a week, with rules being adjusted as experience unfolds.

It is hard to see how such a system could do any harm and it might do a lot of good for the endangered greenbacks and for the unique environment that Boulder hopes to preserve. Even better, it might prevent a worse fate, a sudden political shift in some new City Council that might throw open the area without proper safeguards.

But now let's see what Boulder already has to offer in the way of legal fishing: In addition to its three open reservoirs, Boulder allows catch-and-release fishing in Middle Boulder Creek within the city limits. A minimum stream flow is provided through a program with the Colorado Water Conservation Board.

And while fishing Boulder's open waters—Boulder Reservoir, Barker and Skyscraper—remember that all of Boulder's water, whether open or closed, goes through the same modern treatment process, so fishing poses no threat to water quality.

BOULDER RESERVOIR, 625 surface acres, deepest part 25 ft., altitude 5,173 ft., completed in 1955.

ROAD DIRECTIONS: Boulder Reservoir is located just a few miles northeast of Boulder on Hwy 119. It is well marked on your left.

Three million dollars worth of hard facilities make Boulder Reservoir a major recreational facility, featuring fishing, boating, swimming, water skiing, wind surfing, picnicking and so on. It even has an artificially built sand swimming beach.

All of the major facilities are located on the south shore. If you enter by that gate, there is a day fee that varies according to age. Children six to 12 pay $1.50, ages 13-18 pay $2.25, adults pay $3.50 and seniors over 60 pay $1.50. Boulder residents get a break on season passes and on some activities.

There is no fee for fishing. Fishermen or other visitors can park in five outlying parking lots and walk in from other gates, paying nothing. There is no fee for muscle-powered craft, including float tubes, but gasoline or wind-powered craft do pay fees.

This lake has both warm and cool weather species. It is heavily stocked with catchable rainbows and walleye fry.

Some of the walleye get eaten by other fish, of course, so there aren't a huge number of walleye, but they do get big—up to 15 pounds. One of the staff recently caught one weighing 13 pounds and eight ounces, and several over 12 pounds are caught each year.

The lake also boasts largemouth bass, crappie, sunfish, channel catfish and yellow perch. The yellow perch reach 10 and 12 inches.

Except for the flooded area on the west end, there is not much structure to shelter fish, so the city has been adding structure by stacking Christmas trees on the ice and letting them sink during the thaw. They've been doing this in scattered locations for several years now, adding 400 more this winter alone. Boat fishermen with depth finders will be able to find them.

Water skiers are restricted to a pattern area marked with platforms and buoys to keep from hassling fishermen.

An old regulation cuts down fishing hours during the fall. From Nov. 1 to the end of waterfowl hunting season, the hours are 10 a.m. to 2 p.m., but this reg is now being reviewed and may be dropped. Waterfowl hunting is allowed at Boulder Reservoir, but not at adjacent Coot Lake.

Coot Lake, by the way, is no longer open to nude swimming, darn it, or swimming of any kind. It is also off limits to hunting, but fishing is free.

Boulder Reservoir's main building has showers and lockers and first-aid and concessions. The marina building has more than 50 rental craft available, everything from canoes and rowboats to sailcraft and power fishing boats. You can learn to water ski at the water skiing concession, and the City Parks and Recreation Dept. runs a sailing instruction program. Both on-water and dry-dock boat storage is available with year-round security. Of course, you can also buy gasoline.

This is a day-use area open from 7 a.m. to dark. No dogs are allowed on the south shore between May 15 and Sept. 15. You will be turned away at the main gate if you bring a dog, yet dogs are permitted on a leash on other shores of the lake.

Other rules are typical: No camping, no firearms or fireworks, no glass containers and so forth.

This reservoir remains full all winter, so ice fishing is allowed. The level gradually goes down through August, then starts to rise again, so fluctuations are not huge. The best fishing is in the early spring and late fall.

BARKER RESERVOIR, 190 surface acres, deepest part 80 ft., altitude 8183 ft., completed in 1905.

ROAD DIRECTIONS: Drive up Boulder Canyon to Nederland southwest of Boulder. The road skirts the reservoir as you head into Nederland.

Located in Nederland, Barker is owned and operated by the Public Service Co. of Colorado. but we include it here because it is considered part of Boulder's system.

It's not a great fishing lake because it fluctuates so much and was drained several years ago. No boats are allowed, and its steep banks are hard to walk, especially on the south side. Steep sides also mean no shallow areas, which means less food for the fish. The most accessible bank-fishing area is the inlet.

Catchable rainbows are the mainstay, but Barker has a sucker problem, so splake have been introduced to see if they will eat suckers. (Splake are a sterile cross between brook trout and lake trout.) It's too early to tell if it worked.

SKYSCRAPER RESERVOIR, about 2 or 4 surface acres, deepest part 28 ft., altitude 11,240 ft., completed in 1950.

ROAD DIRECTIONS: Head up Boulder Canyon to Nederland, then go one half mile south on Hwy 72-119. Turn west and go 4 miles to Eldora. Continue one mile on Forest Route 109 to the Hessie Trailhead.

This is Boulder's only high mountain reservoir that is open to the public, but there are many other high lakes in the area that are also open and are not part of Boulder's water system.

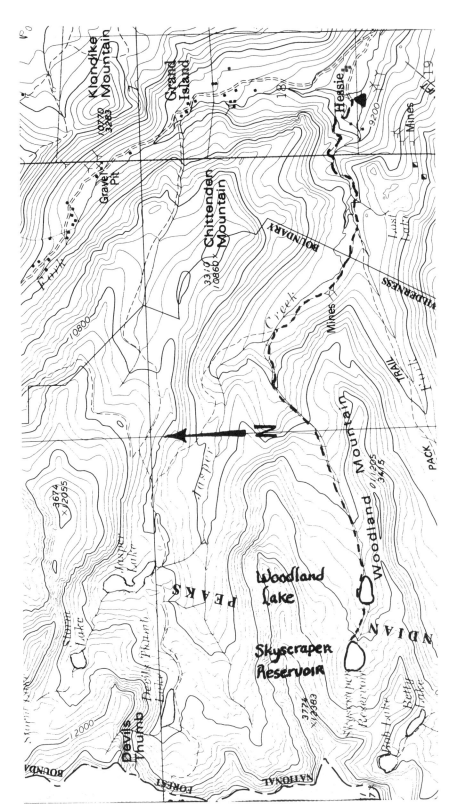

The name says it all. Skyscraper is true Alpine lake perched amid the tundra and rocky heights of the Roosevelt National Forest's Indian Peaks Wilderness, so of course you have to hike or ride horseback to get there. No mountain bicycles allowed.

The trail is good and well marked. Hike west from the Hessie trailhead about 1.5 miles, then take the north fork. Hike up another mile, past mine workings to the next fork, where you turn west. After a two-mile climb, you come to Woodland Lake.

Smaller and only about seven feet deep, Woodland might seem like something to pass up, but **Woodland is one of only two lakes in this book where you can catch grayling!** Hardy volunteers have been backpacking grayling fry to this lake (instead of cutthroat). The work is done chiefly by the Boulder Fish & Game Club, in cooperation with the DOW and the Boulder Flycasters.

Perched at 10,972 feet, a seven-foot-deep lake ought to winter kill, but Woodland's fish take refuge in the stream inlet. Biologists believe this stream is so good that grayling should be able to spawn there.

Volunteer backpackers also stock Skyscraper, which is just a few hundred yards higher at 11,240 feet, but **Skyscraper gets cutthroats.** The best time is just after ice out. Try fishing the shallows near the inlet because that's where the water warms up and where the cutthroat try to spawn. Try using two flies, something light-colored on the end like a parachute Adams to work as an attractor, then tie something dark on a dropper, something like a black gnat or a nymph.

The lake is open to non-motorized boating, so tubers and anglers who pack in inflatable boats do well here.

In August there's a tremendous flying ant hatch, so try to imitate that in a size 14. Like all high lakes, the bite is always boom and bust, furious one moment and dead a few minutes later.

If you're camping in the wilderness, you might want to hop over the ridge to the south to fish Betty and Bob, but DOW Biologist Greg Policky says King Lake is better. There is no official trail that crosses this ridge, so **tread lightly where there is tundra.**

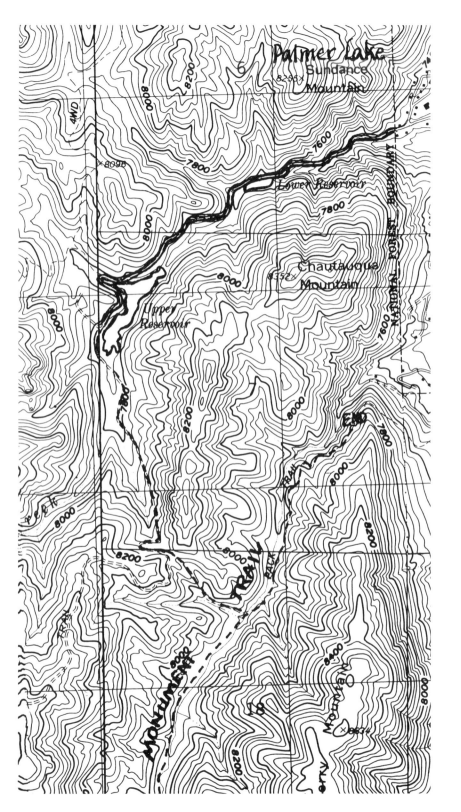

CITY OF PALMER LAKE RESERVOIRS
1 Open to All
1 Closed

Upper Reservoir (Open)
Lower Reservoir (Closed)

Named after its downtown fishing lake, Palmer Lake also has two reservoirs in the woods above town. But while we're at it, we should mention that the 20-acre lake downtown is open from 5 a.m. to 11 p.m. and has the usual state fishing regulations, including bait fishing. Originally, this spring-fed lake was called Loch Katrine, but in 1883 both it and the town were renamed in honor of General William Jackson Palmer, whose railroad made it all possible.

El Paso County Parks and Recreation has also established the trailhead for the new Santa Fe Trail at the city lake's park. This trail leads through the Air Force Academy.

The reservoirs, however, are located in the rocky forest canyon of North Monument Creek, a very scenic place. On the way. you'll pass The Estemere, estate of town-founder Dr. William Finley Thompson. This Victorian gingerbread mansion, completed in 1887, will soon be an art gallery.

Palmer Lake's watershed is open for day-use without special permits, so long as you obey the various rules that are not all detailed on a single sign: no firearms, no horses, no motor vehicles, no camping, no swimming, no persons or pets in the water and so on. Do not block the gate. A squeeze-through entryway is provided at gateside so you won't have to climb over the gate.

ROAD DIRECTIONS: Take I-25 to the Monument-Palmer Lake Exit and head toward the mountains. You'll soon pass the Palmer Lake city limits sign, but downtown is three miles beyond that. Watch for the Villa restaurant on your right and turn left there onto Glenway (not Middle or Lower Glenway), and go straight—slowly—past the school and past The Estemere. Your road dead-ends at the watershed gate. Parking is next to the filter plant on your right. Parking is very limited (three or four cars), but don't block the gate or plant doors.

LOWER RESERVOIR, less than two surface acres, deepest point 12 ft., altitude 7,600 ft., rebuilt in 1903.

Once you've seen what awaits you upstream, this pond will seem insignificant!

And with so little parking available—or even possible—to serve both lakes, this smallest and shallowest reservoir might stay closed to fishing. At the time of this writing, its fish had been flushed downstream by a recent draining. A chain link fence cuts it off from the road that leads to the Upper Reservoir, but a narrow path along part of the opposite shore suggests that some sneak-ins have given it a try. The narrow dam is gated off to prevent entry. The penalty for trespassing is a fine up to $300 or 90 days in jail.

Just stay on the road and walk a little farther. You won't be disappointed.

UPPER RESERVOIR, about 10 surface acres, deepest point 38 ft., altitude 7,760 ft., built in 1903.

Located less than a mile from the filter plant gate, Upper Reservoir is a scenic lake where you can hike and fish and walk a dog, so long as it stays strictly out of the water. Your dog must be on a leash or under your verbal control. There are no picnic tables, but roughing-it picnickers are welcome.

At the time of this writing, Upper Reservoir was awaiting its first load of stocker trout after being drained three years in a row for repairs. It seems that excavations to provide proper footing for a new membrane on the dam accidentally broke into a natural fissure in the granite formation on the far side of the dam. So when the lake refilled, it started to leak, gushing from rocks well below the dam. Fixing that proved difficult. It finally took six loads of concrete pumped underground until concrete began gushing from the same opening below the dam.

The dam itself is a narrow curving wall built by the Corps of Engineers. It is so strong that it stood up to the flood of 1965, when five feet of water poured over the top.

As you hike the road, you first cross the inlet of Cave Creek. The same flood of '65 apparently rearranged the boulders that once gave this creek it's name. At the far end of the lake, where photographers will find their best vantage point, that flood made a gravel delta that robbed the lake of part of its capacity. Most of the time, it's easy to cross the creek in the willow areas. A shoreline fishing trail skirts much of the reservoir, mostly on the far side.

Don't wade without waders. A metal sign spells out most of the rules: "Palmer Lake Watershed. This is Our Drinking Water. No camping. No person or pets in water. No littering or polluting. Remove Your Own Trash. Violators Subject to $300 fine or 90 days in Jail."

The National Forest begins just a few yards from the lake, and you'll see evidence that people thought they could camp there. Yet the slopes on both sides are all part of the watershed, even though it is federal, and all watershed rules apply, including no camping, no open fires, no horses, no motor vehicles and so on. Mountain bicycles are being tried on a temporary basis and give access to the trail that leads over the hill to Limbaugh Canyon. See the *Trails Guide*, pg. 119, Monument Trail.

Oddly enough, the people who mistakenly and illegally camped here did some service for the forest, for the woods are now clear of dead wood, which so often endangers other closed areas.

If repairs hold this time, Upper Reservoir may be stocked with catchable sized trout in 1993 or 94. (They want to make sure it doesn't leak again.) Brook trout from the stream above will doubtless begin to fatten up here also.

Biologists say this lake has good potential. Retiring Road and Water Supervisor Bob Schroeder knows it does: **"When we first drained Upper Reservoir, we found trout 15 and 18 inches long!"**

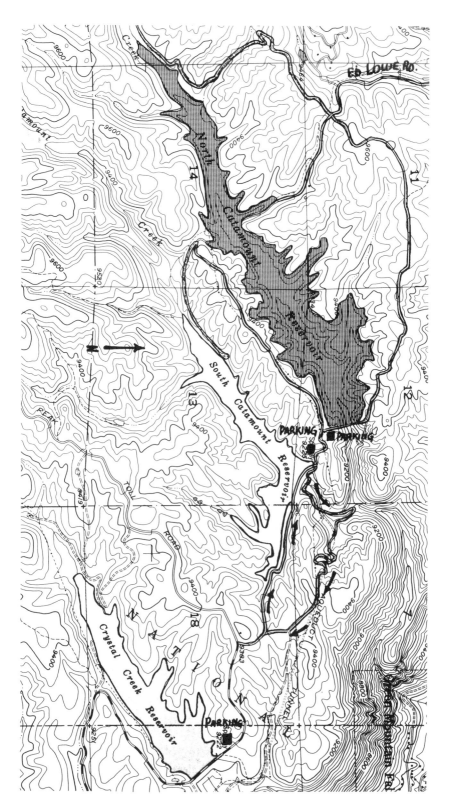

COLORADO SPRINGS LAKES
10 Open to All (2 Have No Fish)
8 Still Closed to All (2 Have No Fish)
1 Open to Some

3 North Slope Lakes—NEWLY OPENED
9 South Slope Lakes
4 Rampart (Northfield) Lakes
3 Outlying Lakes

The engineers never meant for the fishing to be so good: They just couldn't help it.

Growth was the real motive. Without water, small towns remain small, but Colorado Springs grew to become the state's second largest city because of water stored in the mountains.

Like Denver, Colorado Springs operates a far-flung water empire stretching beyond the Continental Divide. Indeed, Colorado Springs is destined to grow to a population of half a million because it already has enough water to support yet another hundred thousand people. An aggressive Utility Dept. has made this growth possible.

Yet almost as a by-product, this empire also represents an exciting collection of recreational treasures, mountain lakes as beautiful as they are valuable, scenic wonderlands jumping with trout, a postcard land of evergreens and wildflowers and majestic rocks under a sapphire sky.

Quite a few people think this is all too good to waste behind "No Trespassing" signs, so Colorado Springs is beginning to open its watershed lakes. The newest reservoirs were built open: Homestake, Montgomery and Rampart. As an experiment, a closed lake was opened in 1984, and in 1992, three more were opened on the North Slope. Future improvements may lead to opening more as well, giving Colorado Springs a far-flung fishing empire that will draw tourists as well as locals.

It's a big system, so we'll take it in sections, but before we start, remember that locked gates and special permit requirements make Bighorn and Wilson "closed," even though they have no fish. But Stratton and Upper Blue require no special permits, so we list them as "open," even though they have no fish and no possibilities.

COLORADO SPRINGS PIKES PEAK NORTH SLOPE LAKES 3 NOW OPEN TO ALL

Crystal Reservoir (Open)
South Catamount Reservoir (Open)
North Catamount Reservoir (Open)

After a year of planning and generations of closure, three of the largest lakes on America's most famous mountain opened to the public in 1992. Crystal and North Catamount and South Catamount have so many fish they needed no stocking before opening, but stocking did begin quickly at Crystal in anticipation of heavy pressure. All have their own charm, and each offers a different recreational experience. They also happen to be very beautiful, now the crown jewels of the city's park system.

Way back in 1967, the people of Colorado Springs voted three to one to open these lakes on the North Slope of Pikes Peak just as soon as the Ute Pass communities received fully treated water. "No one ever thought it would take this long!" moaned Attorney Sandy Kraemer, author of the referendum. Cascade couldn't afford a modern filter plant, so in the fall of 1990, Colorado Springs began supplying filtered water to Cascade.

All three lakes have a special combined limit of four fish, only one of which can be a lake trout and only if the laker is over 20 inches long. Bait is allowed at Crystal and at South

Catamount, but only artificial flies and lures may be used at North Catamount. Of course, a valid Colorado fishing license is required.

The 20-inch requirement for lake trout is a good-news-bad-news situation. The good news is that DOW samplings have historically shown that the average lake trout on the North Slope is about 20 inches long. So you would have a good chance of catching a keeper mackinaw. But the bad news is that no boating or floatation devices are allowed for the Phase I opening, and since lake trout are deep water fish, you have little chance of landing a keeper until the floatation rules change in a later phase of the park's development.

Smaller laker trout do come near shore in the spring right after ice off, but generally big ones stay shy of bank fishermen, and some genuine lunkers lurk in these waters! Nobody knows how big some might be, but when the DOW goes sampling, they net lake trout over 30 inches long and weighing about ll pounds!

One limiting factor for boaters would be the Pikes Peak Hwy. itself, which does not currently allow any kind of trailer. So unless Ed Lowe Road (correct spelling) becomes a viable access, any boat coming up the highway would have to be on top of your car. Even belly boats would help, since the usual method for taking mackinaw is to jig for them on the bottom.

But the good news is that the Utility Dept. does not oppose boating. There is more opposition to the noise of boats because the park is such a serene area. But the City of Aurora came up with a successful program to rent boats with quiet electric motors at two reservoirs they opened. Indeed, at both Aurora lakes those programs paid for the boats and motors within the first season!

Ice fishing is also banned for 1992.

Eventually, planners envision a regional park involving two county governments as well as the city, but **for 1992, recreation is limited to bank fishing, hiking and picnicking. This is only Phase 1 of an experimental project, so please be considerate.**

Most area service roads are closed to public vehicles, but are open to hiking. So you may drive to the lake of your choice, leave your vehicle in a parking lot near the dam and hike from there, either following the bank or hiking roads. **Please do not** park along the road on the way in: Please use the parking lots only.

Planners hope to build a system of mountain bicycle trails to link with the service roads, giving anglers the chance to pedal to the far end of a lake. Since this is a day-use area—and a very big one—mountain bikes could greatly increase the amount of time you could spend fishing remote areas. Yet without trails designed for mountain bikes, the concern is that bikes might be used along shores, which might greatly increase erosion.

Unless Ed Lowe Road from Woodland Park can be greatly improved, driving to the North Slope will mean taking the Pikes Peak Toll Road. It costs $5 per person to go to the summit (kids aged five and under free), but a reduced toll means that **North Slope users will pay $2 each, with kids aged 15 and under free.** Only part of your fee goes to the North Slope project: The rest is toll. But if you pay $2, **don't be tempted to cheat and drive to the top of the mountain or you'll be caught on the way down** at Glenn Cove, where you must stop so officers can check your brakes. **If you go to the top, you are required to hang your ticket from the rear-view mirror to show which fee you paid.**

And don't try to use Ed Lowe Road. It has serious safety problems. If it were just a fishing road, Ed Lowe might be fine, but since it is the only access for a residential area—and a terrible one at that—any increase in traffic may wind up hurting a station-wagon load of kids, so **a special enforcement effort is underway to keep North Slope visitors away. There is no public parking along Ed Lowe Road, and the residents are very alert!** If Ed Lowe and its dangerous intersection at Hwy. 24 are improved, this may become the major access, which may also lower the fee.

Although fishing is regulated by the DOW, other North Slope recreation is managed by the Colorado Springs Parks and Recreation Dept. and a ranger is on duty. This is a major change because Parks and Rec. has generally stayed within the city limits, having no presence at other open lakes in the city's system. This is a great relief to the Utility Dept., which has never wanted to be in the Parks and Recreation business.

You can help expand your freedoms by respecting park rules and its amenities, by treating the place as a living muse-

um where the wildlife and wildflowers and other natural fea-
tures remain undisturbed. Please keep noise to a minimum,
control your kids and make sure pets stay strictly on leash. (Dogs
chasing wildlife led to a complete ban at Florissant. Dogs in our
drinking water might also lead to a ban.) No swimming or wading or other body contact is allowed. Cook only with charcoal,
never wood, and only in established fire grates. No firearms, no
fireworks, no littering. You may blanket picnic in remote areas,
but in popular areas, please use the tables. Large groups are especially encouraged to use designated areas.

Ribbon cutting in 1992 was delayed because of parking lot
construction, but in normal years the season should run between
early May and mid October. The toll gate's opening and closing
varies, so telephone (719) 684-9383 for current times. In summer
gates open at 7 a.m. and you must leave before the Toll Gate locks
at 8:30 p.m., which means making your last cast around 7:30
because it takes awhile to drive down. After Labor Day, hours
shorten: 9 a.m. to 5 p.m., but please start packing up by 4 p.m.

Access is free for those who earn it with their feet. You may
hike in (a long way) from the Crags or Green Mountain Falls.
(Please note: Another old path from Chipita Park trespasses on
private property.) These very primitive paths are not officially
designated, not well marked and cannot be officially recommended. Newcomers will find it easy to get lost!

**For hike-in anglers, the big change is this: You will no
longer be arrested for being there in daylight. But you may
not fish at night or camp overnight on the watershed, even if it
is part of federal land. At night you are still a trespasser,** and
now a ranger as well as the caretaker will be looking for you.

For example, you could backpack to the Crags, camp outside
of the watershed at the headwaters of Fourmile Creek, then hike
in to fish in daylight and return to your camp in the evening.
There are beaver ponds along South Catamount creek before you
ever get to the reservoir itself. Just know that it is a very long trek
and make sure you leave watershed property before nightfall
Signs, if not fences, mark the boundaries. For directions to the
Crags, see the *Trails Guide* pg. 87.

Another hike-in route begins at the Thomas Trail in Green

Mountain Falls and climbs up beyond Catamount Falls, following Catamount Creek. This is a killer climb, very narrow and not at all the kind of place to take the kids. Dick Bratton of Green Mountain Falls is working to improve signs. For directions to the Thomas Trail which begins this trek, see the *Trails Guide*, pg. 65.

ROAD DIRECTIONS: From I-25, take the Manitou-Pikes Peak Exit and drive west on Hwy 24 for 9.5 miles. The entrance to the North Pole and Pikes Peak Highway is a well-marked left turn across traffic at Cascade. The toll gate is half a mile beyond. Six miles beyond the gate, the highway crosses the dam of CRYSTAL RESERVOIR. Parking is on your left just across the dam. To find the CATAMOUNTS, go another 0.6 miles on the toll road and find the turnoff on your right. This gravel road has a one-way loop system leading to parking lots below the dams of SOUTH CATAMOUNT and NORTH CATAMOUNT. Just beyond the gate you take the left fork and follow signs. PARK ONLY IN LOTS.

CRYSTAL RESERVOIR, 106 surface acres, deepest part 55 ft., altitude 9,222 ft., built in 1935

Crystal has been flirting with visitors for generations. Locals and tourists of the world have always rubber-necked as they drove along her long dam on their way to the summit. Crystal sprawls in full view, with no hidden arms, a wide pool as inviting as a postcard and with a close-up view of Pikes Peak as her backdrop. How many visitors must have a snapshot of Crystal!

Even before her first stocking, Crystal sported a large population of 10-inch brook trout and some good-sized lakers, but the DOW has allocated thousands of catchable rainbows to keep her catch-rate up, so Crystal should remain alluring season after season.

Crystal's northern banks (the parking lot side) are gentle and grassy, so it's a great place for kids. The opposite side of the lake, however, is steep and unwalkable in places. Please help prevent erosion by staying away from that side unless a trail is provided. The shoreline measures about 3.3 miles.

Picnic tables and restrooms are available near the parking lot.

Wheelchair access facilities are also in the works.

Most of Crystal's original fish are brook trout, but its minority population of lakers is doing well. Trouble is, without boats to access the deep water where lakers live, you don't have much chance of catching one during the Phase I opening. Remember the special limit is four fish, only one of which can be a laker and the laker has to be over 20 inches. Bait fishing is allowed at Crystal.

DOW samplings net brookies averaging close to 10 inches, with the largest being over 12 inches. Years ago the DOW introduced a few lake trout to Crystal as an experiment. Sampling show that lakers are a minority population, but Crystal's lakers average around 20 inches. Fishing from the dam is banned.

SOUTH CATAMOUNT RESERVOIR, 93 surface acres, deepest part 65ft., altitude 9,225 ft., built in 1937.

Of the three sister lakes, South Catamount has the richest nutrients and the largest population of wild fish. It also has the most complex shoreline, just a little steeper than North Cat, but still mostly walkable (the shoreline measures about four miles). The worst spot is a scree slope right across from the southern end of the dam, so if you fish that side you'll have to hike up and around that cove. Trails are being planned.

The north shore is the easiest walking, but the fastest way to reach the the far end of the lake is to hike the access road that traces the ridge between North and South Cat. Starting next to the North Cat dam, this road leads back 1.1 miles to a four-way intersection. The road ahead leads only a short distance to an overlook with a view of North Cat. Turning right at the intersection takes you immediately down to North Cat. Turning left, however, takes you to the South Catamount Creek inlet, then doubles back for a short distance along South Cat's upper shore. Distance to the end of this spur: half a mile.

Glancing at the map, you might imagine this big inlet area to be muddy and boggy, but instead it is solid gravel. Even in spring, you'll find it fairly easy to cross the converging creeks at this gravel delta area and start back around the other side of the lake on a game-and-sneak-in fisherman's path.

The south shore is walkable, though a little steeper, and is interrupted by inlets where the brook trout should go to spawn in September. Tread carefully around South Cat, however, because this lake already has an erosion problem stemming from dust and runoff from the unpaved portion of the Pikes Peak Highway. Sometimes South Cat is turbid when the other two are clear. Paving the highway and rehabbing the old ski area might do a great deal for South Cat in the long run.

South Cat's brook trout are fat and sassy, perhaps kept in check by big brookie cannibals. The DOW's samplings net brookies averaging about 11 inches, with the largest measuring over 15 inches. Fishing from the dam is banned because it's steel face is so steep that anyone who fell in would have a hard time climbing out.

NORTH CATAMOUNT RESERVOIR, 261 surface acres, deepest point 135 ft., altitude 9,440 ft., built in 1960.

North Cat is your trophy lake, home of the biggest fish on Pikes Peak itself, lake trout measuring over 30 inches. The DOW rarely stocks closed reservoirs, but since this area was due for eventual opening, the division stocked lake trout in North Cat years ago. The result is a population backwards from that at Crystal, mostly lakers with a few brookies. On average, North Cat's brookies are bigger and fatter than Crystal's. **Fishing is by artificial fly and lure only**.

Every bit of North Cat's shoreline is walkable. The scree-looking area across from the dam is actually a gravel beach left over from mining gravel for the dam. Unfortunately, the access road that skirts its north shore loops out a long way from the water, so it takes awhile to hike down to the northern coves. Starting at the dam, that road goes back two miles to a major intersection with concrete utility works in the middle. Going to the right there leads to Ed Lowe Road. Going left leads 0.6 miles down to the lake's biggest cove where water gushes from an underground pipeline leading from Montgomery Reservoir on

Hoosier Pass. This cove is a great place to fish, according to unnamed sources.

Going straight ahead from the big intersection leads another 1.5 miles to the upper end of the lake (3.5 miles from the dam). The shore is gentle and grassy where the road skirts the lake, a nice spot for a blanket picnic. Notice the game-and-sneak-in fisherman's path across the lake, snaking along close to the high water mark. You'll have to go father up the road to cross the inlet creek to access that trail.

However, the best access to the south shore of North Cat is the ridge road described in South Cat's section. If you hike the shore all the way around, the distance is about 6.6 miles.

If you continue up the valley we've been describing for another half mile, you'll come to stream gate area where satellite transmission gear keeps tabs on North Catamount Creek's flow. South Catamount Creek has the same satellite gear.

The DOW's samplings net many more lakers than brookies at North Cat. The lakers average about 20 inches, with the biggest measuring over 30 inches. Intensive sampling, will begin this summer and continue to keep tabs of the population. The state mackinaw record is 42 inches, weighing 36 pounds.

North Catamount has fewer brookies than South Cat, but they are bigger. The samples average about 14 inches, with the largest measuring over 15 inches. By the way, brookies over 15 inches start bulking up instead of growing much longer. The state record is seven pounds and 10 ounces.

Since lakers dominate North Cat, the DOW is hoping for boats. Otherwise North Cat's biggest fish are going to be out of reach most of the time until rules change. But there's good news: Unlike the other two North Slope lakes, fishing is allowed from North Cat's dam, your best way to access deep water. This is a good place to try for lake trout in October, when the lakers approach rip-rap in an attempt to spawn. Fishing from the dam is banned in the other two lakes.

COLORADO SPRINGS PIKES PEAK SOUTH SLOPE

Penrose-Rosemont (Open)
McReynolds Reservoir #5 (Closed)
Mason Reservoir #4 (Closed)
Boehmer Reservoir #(Closed)
Bighorn Reservoir #7 (Closed, But No Fish)
Wilson Reservoir #8 ((Closed, But No Fish)
Lake Moraine (Closed)
Big Tooth Reservoir #1 (Closed)
Stratton Reservoir (Open, But No Fish)

A land of legendary monsters and very real whoppers, the South Slope of Pikes Peak sports the largest collection of lakes in the Colorado Springs water system. A few of them are visible from the summit of Pikes Peak, blue gems in the distance. For generations riders of the Pikes Peak Cog Railway have pressed their faces against the windows and drooled at some of them, while a guide intoned the usual warning that the area remains off-limits. Some have no fish, but most are jumping.

The big news is that one lake in this general area is now open and there is talk, at least, of opening more, so long as prudent preparations are made. The South Slope presents some special concerns for everyone involved. Watershed managers are concerned about fire hazard and the DOW is concerned about protecting special habitats for bighorn sheep and cutthroat trout. But there are opportunities here.

Here's a place where fire-preventers did too good a job. Without small fires (or campers) to burn up dead wood, some areas gradually filled up with dry fuel. In some places, a dead tree has no place to fall, instead simply leaning against another, producing a dangerous thicket of fuel.

In hindsight, it now seems that generations of "No Trespassing" may have helped to endanger the watershed instead of simply protecting it. The future health of this forest depends upon human help, not human exclusion.

Yet solutions involves risk. Foresters worry that an influx of visitors might increase the danger of touching off a blaze. Controlled burns may be uncontrollable here, so fuel wood must be cleaned out by hand. Free permits for gathering firewood can be obtained from Don Mulligan's office. See WHAT ABOUT FIRE DANGER? in our final chapter for permit details.

Some of these lakes are very special to the DOW itself. One is home to a pure strain of a threatened species, Colorado's only surviving native trout, the Type A greenback cutthroat. Two others have been used to supply eggs and milt for hatching other cutthroats. The hatching is done in Salida or Leadville, and surprisingly, the offspring are brought back to their parent lakes as well as being used to stock other waters.

"Most high lakes don't have suitable habitat or conditions for trout spawning, with the possible exception of brook trout." says DOW biologist Douglas Krieger. "We actually have to restock these brood lakes."

"Leave it alone" has always been the easiest policy for protecting these resources, but since the division is legally bound to seek opportunities, officers keep wondering if there isn't a way to open South Slope lakes someday on a restricted basis. After all, the division doesn't breed trout so that no one can catch them. Furthermore, not all of the lakes are brood lakes, so what about the others?

Obviously, considering the lakes individually will help develop policies that better fit the area, for there has always been a tendency to lump everything together.

One of the highest lakes, Stratton, has been drained because of an unsafe dam and the resulting puddle is so shallow that it winterkills, so it won't be discussed further. We count it as "open" only because nobody tries to keep you out.

ROAD DIRECTIONS: *Penrose-Rosemont is not part of the South Slope Water System, but is located on the peak's south slope. Its park-*

*ing lot is located on the Gold Camp Road only 3.5 miles uphill from
the popular St. Peter's Dome overlook.*

*Except for STRATTON RESERVOIR, the seven other lakes can only by
reached via Forest Service Access Road #376 from the Gold Camp
Road. The entrance is much closer to Cripple Creek than it is to
Colorado Springs. From I-25, take the Manitou-Pikes Peak Exit #141
and drive Hwy 24 west to Divide. Turn left onto 67 and go about 15
miles to a high plains bend in the road called Gillett (no town), where
you go straight ahead on gravel instead of continuing on pavement to
Cripple Creek. When you reach the Gold Camp, make a hairpin left
turn and drive about five miles. Just past Cathedral Park (where it
looks like the rocks were still sticking to God's fingers when he pulled
away), you'll find #376 on your left. Somebody keeps knocking down
the marker post, so watch your odometer and remember that #376 follows the next creek that crosses the road after Cathedral Park. Many
visitors don't know that there are primitive undeveloped campsites in
the National Forest along this road, which is finally blocked by a stur-
dy Utility Dept. gate. YOU MAY FISH THE CREEK OUTSIDE OF
THIS FENCE (small trout), BUT DON'T BLOCK THE GATE. Level
ground here may lend itself to the construction of a parking lot for a
walk-in situation in the future.*

PENROSE-ROSEMONT RESERVOIR, 77 surface acres, deep-
est point 87 ft., altitude 9,600 ft., built in 1932, enlarged in
'62.

Now open to everyone, Penrose-Rosemont used to be the
private fishing hole of the rich and famous. Before being sold
to Colorado Springs, this beautiful lake served guests of the
five-star Broadmoor Hotel and the Spencer Penrose family.
Celebrities like Boxing Champ Jack Dempsey were pho-
tographed angling here.

More tourists carry home snapshots of this lake than any other
in the Colorado Spring system, for it can be seen from several
angles along the Gold Camp Road and looks glorious during
aspen season. The chain link fence and its "No Trespassing" signs
still stand, but the lake is **now open to fishing only** and no special
permit is required.

This is one reservoir where you can be arrested for NOT
fishing! Imagine the irony. A decade ago, anyone caught near

this lake with a fishing rod was in big trouble, but when my wife and I first walked down just to look at it, after working for years to open it to fishing, the caretaker busted us for not fishing! He let us go when he saw that we had valid fishing licenses, which proved that we had helped to pay for DOW improvements there, but he warned us that we must not return without fishing gear. That's why **the trailhead sign says, "Trail for Use of Fishermen Only."**

We hadn't seen the final draft of the lease, which only allows fishing and specifically bans such things as picnicking. Here's the list of other no-nos: No hiking, no picnicking, no dogs, no horses, no mountain bicycles or motorized vehicles, no skiing, no camping, no fires, no wading, no swimming or water body contact of any kind; no boating, no floatation devices of any kind, no firearms or fireworks, no alcohol, no ice fishing and no bait fishing.

Most of these rules can be found at any open reservoir, but the rest are designed to limit human impact to fishing only. Anglers paid for all of the improvements at the lake by buying fishing licenses. The lake is small and very close to a popular tourist road. It's parking lot is tiny (only enough room for about a dozen vehicles), so it would soon fill up with non-fishing tourists, leaving no room for the anglers who pay the bills.

So if you want to picnic here, be sure that everyone in your party has fishing gear and everyone 15 years of age or over has a valid Colorado fishing license. That makes it legal.

Opening this lake was a triumph of cooperation. A broadly-based citizens group called the Pikes Peak Committee for Freer Use of Public Lands quietly negotiated behind closed doors with three governments. The result was the first experimental opening of a closed reservoir in the Colorado Springs system in many years.

The city provided legal work. The DOW provided concrete vault restrooms and litter barrels and pays to service them. The DOW also provided liability insurance and stocks the lake and helps to patrol it. The Forest Service was not actually a signatory to the deal, but cooperated by building the short access trail and creatively mining gravel across the road to produce the parking lot.

The only hitch was a leak in the dam. Soon after opening in 1984, the lake had to be drained and was dry for years. But in 1991 it was ready again and restocked, first with rainbows and then with Snake River cutthroats. Brookies have already moved in from the stream above and are already being taken in the 10-inch range, so they are expected to keep growing. There is no sucker problem at present and pressure from trout may keep them down. In fact, lake trout are also being considered. All in all, **this lake has wonderful potential.**

"You should've come with us!" Greg Kelley told me over the phone. "We caught our limit in 30 minutes!"

The trail from the Gold Camp Road is short and easy, well under a half mile, and the shoreline trail is almost flat. Do not approach the dam, the caretaker's house or private property on the north side of the lake. A fence and sign about halfway along the northwest edge mark where you must stop. The trail on the southeast side goes almost all the way to the dam.

A day-use area, the lake is open from 5:30 a.m. to 9 p.m. Due to icing, the lake is open generally from May 11 to October 31. **Fishing is by flies and artificial lures only.** Both the DOW and a resident caretaker patrol the area. Please help by reporting violations and by encouraging your guests to be on their best behavior. Your cooperation may help open other such areas in the future.

McREYNOLDS RESERVOIR #5, 100 surface acres, deepest point 37 ft., altitude 10,960 ft., built in 1905.

—AND—

MASON RESERVOIR #5, 107 surface acres, deepest point 33 ft., altitude 10,960 ft., built in 1905.

These twin sisters are so alike we're going to describe them together. Maps call this the Seven Lakes area, and since there are so many lakes on the South Slope, people get confused trying to figure out which ones make the seven. Actually, these two lakes are all that are left of the original seven lakes that gave this basin its name. Years ago they were consolidated by engineers, so there are now only two lakes at Seven Lakes.

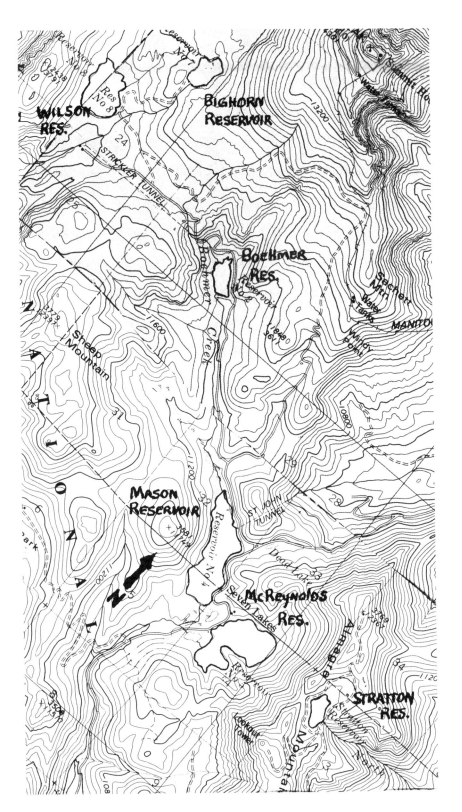

These reservoirs occupy a wide open valley with the nearest trees along the northeast side. The caretaker lives full time on the bend of the road between them, so the place is well watched! The ease with which the caretaker can see what's going on here is often mentioned during discussions about opening the area.

Both lakes are still a useful source of eggs and milt for cutthroat trout, despite the fact that the gene pools in these pools have become terribly confused. "Pikes Peak cutthroat" come solely from these two lakes. The term is only meant to distinguish these fish from those taken from Trapper Lake and is not really meant to describe a different strain, but unfortunately, **Pikes Peak cutthroat are not the pure Type A greenback cutthroat now so highly protected as a threatened species.**

This illustrates one of the nightmares faced by biologists when contemplating opening "hatchery lakes" to fishing. Managers are often as worried about somebody putting fish in as they are about anglers taking fish out of such lakes. *Never release a fish where it doesn't belong. Don't let your kids release a fish from one place into another, even if the lakes are only a few feet apart, as they are here.* You can really screw up the biology, and that's a mistake the division likes to make all by itself.

Many years ago, when cutthroats were not well understood, the DOW thought that pure greenbacks were gone. In trying to save some kind of cutthroat, the division experimented and used what it had. Yellowstone and Colorado River cutthroats were mixed with greenbacks in these lakes. Indeed, a few Snake River cutthoats were also added to McReynolds, but not to Mason.

The result is a mixed breed, still highly prized, though biologists are careful to keep them separate from pure strains. Biologists have been sorting them for years now, removing any Snake Rivers, for example, so now they all look very much like greenbacks.

"If you hold up two fish side by side, they may look pretty much identical," says biologist Douglas Krieger. "But we don't want them mixed because its very important to preserve genetics as best we can. Even the potential of a mixture drops the strain into a different class (Class B), even if you can't prove that any actual mixing was done. Because of the Snake Rivers, we don't even want fish from McReynolds put into Mason just across the road."

Even though you can't fish for these cutthroats here, you can catch them elsewhere right now. After being hatched and reared in Salida, they are stocked in high lakes of the Collegiate and Sangre de Cristo mountains. You can also find them at Montgomery Reservoir (see CS Outlying Lakes). On the peak itself, you can fish for these cutthroat on Fourmile Creek along the DOW's Dome Rock Trail. See *Trails Guide* pg. 94.

Apparently the habitat at Mason and McReynolds is not quite good enough to allow cutthroats to reproduce naturally in large enough numbers to sustain the population, so these lakes are continually restocked. No actual census numbers have been gathered yet, but cutthroats netted at Mason run from 11 to 15 inches. McReynolds cutthroats are larger, 12 to 18 inches!

Larger fish and more convenient working conditions make McReynolds the division's favorite for gathering eggs and milt. Mason has not been used at all in recent years.

What the division envisions is a controlled walk-in situation, where you would leave your car at the gate and walk across the valley to the lakes. Flies and lures would be required, because bait-caught fish too often swallow hooks. A parking lot, restrooms and fire-control measures would be required—along with city approval. But if all that could be done, the fishing could be spectacular because cutthroat have an exciting quality called high catch rate. Which means they like to bite. You may have to put them back, but you could have a great time catching them. Even if opened, these lakes might be closed for a week each summer during DOW milt and egg collection.

BOEHMER RESERVOIR #2, 25 surface acres, deepest point 35 ft., altitude 11,360, built in 1894.

Boehmer is even more precious to the DOW because it is stocked with pure-strain Type A greenback cutthroats. This species will remain on the threatened list until 20 habitats can be established where the fish breed naturally without influence from other breeds. If the fish at Boehmer are successful at raising families, Boehmer may work out to be one of those 20 habitats. Biologists might know as early as the fall of 1992. The big question is whether or not the greenbacks will be able to sustain themselves naturally without the constant restocking required elsewhere. So far, conditions look good.

Mind you, the Utility Dept. is not at all anxious to recommend opening Boehmer, but the DOW would certainly consider it, probably on a catch-and-release basis. (You can already fish for type-A greenbacks on a catch-and-release basis at a number of Colorado lakes, including Lytle Pond at Fort Carson, where many special permits are available to the general public.)

So far, the city has been extremely cooperative with the DOW experiment. They drained the lake at the DOW's request and allowed the division to use a chemical to kill off any remaining fish. (It's not often that you can talk watershed managers into using retenone on a reservoir.) And, of course, they try to keep the lake full, though the primary purpose of any reservoir is drinking water, not fish breeding.

Located at 11,400 feet, Boehmer is well above timberline and is surrounded by delicate tundra that can be damaged just by walking on it. It should be noted that tundra itself does not keep other high mountain lakes closed, but if you get a special permit to hike this area, please keep in mind that such lakes generally have established trails, thus minimizing damage. Any scar on tundra can take a century to grow back, so if you can find a path, please stay on it.

BIGHORN RESERVOIR #7, 37 surface acres, deepest part 18 ft., altitude 11,920 ft., built in 1896.
—AND—
WILSON RESERVOIR #8, 91 surface acres, deepest part 19 ft., altitude 11, 760 ft., built in 1896.

Again, these twin sisters have so much in common that we'll describe them together. They share a common problem, too—no fish! These lakes illustrate the difference between natural lakes and reservoirs in a mountain system.

A reservoir can be very much like a natural lake, eventually having the same kind of ecology, but only if water levels remain somewhat constant. Yet reservoirs have something different—plumbing.

The sapphire necklace of lakes on Pikes Peak is strung together by pipelines. In the winter, when runoff turns to ice and no longer replenishes the water supply, the highest lake (Bighorn) drains to keep the next lake full (Wilson). Then Wilson drains to keep Boehmer full. This leaves almost nothing behind but an ice cap, so you can write off Bighorn and Wilson as fisheries. They are better places to view wildlife.

As Bighorn's name suggests, these lakes are the home base of the Pikes Peak bighorn herd, which numbered 225 in the 1992 census. Bighorns were once extinct on Pikes Peak, so years ago the DOW transplanted a small band from the Buffalo Peaks area. "They're doing fine," says specialist Mark Elkins of the DOW.

They have quite a range. Bighorn wearing the Pikes Peak tag are seen along the Gold Camp, across 67 at Dome Rock and have even been identified at the NORAD gate on Cheyenne Mountain! They lamb in late May, but don't necessarily lamb at their lakeside home base, generally preferring lower altitude hideaways such as Bottomless Pit, which is open to hikers.

In general, bighorn quickly adapt to people who seem harmless and who are doing something predictable, something they've seen before. They certainly don't seem to mind the heavy equipment rumbling at quarries near Queen's Canyon.

These lakes are quite high—Wilson at 11,650 ft. and Bighorn at 12,000—so if you obtain a special permit to hike here, remember how delicate the tundra is and try to stick to established paths. An abandoned road shortcuts between the two lakes.

The stream below Wilson offers great beaver pond fishing in the National Forest, but DO NOT TRESPASS on City of Victor property located farther downstream. You may fish for brookies in beaver ponds upstream from Victor's property, but look out because there is no fence and a full time enforcement officer is watching for trespassers.

LAKE MORAINE, 85 surface acres, deepest part 31 ft., altitude 10,210 ft., natural glacial lake re-engineered in 1891.

Legend holds that a monster lives in Lake Moraine, something like a sea serpent or a Pikes Peak version of the Loch Ness Monster. This critter sprang from the imagination of the U.S. Army Signal Corps., who found their post on top of Pikes Peak a rather lonely duty. What interests most anglers are the legendary fish that lurk there today. When I visited, they were biting at bark tossed into the water!

Many consider Lake Moraine to be the crown jewel of the area, and it is certainly one of the prettiest. It's distinctive shape, including a long spit projecting into deep water, makes it easy to identify even from the summit of Pikes Peak.

This is one reservoir that has no construction date because it was actually scooped out by a glacier eons ago. Moraine is a term for the hill of debris pushed by a glacier, and that is how this lake's dam was formed. However, it is not entirely natural, for engineers long ago dredged it to make it deeper. You can still find tall piles of peat moss in the woods near the lake, material taken out during the dredging.

Lake Moraine used to be the site of a hotel. Tourists would ride mules up the Bear Creek Trail, spend the night at Moraine and then continue to the summit the next day. Like other quaint old tourist hotels, it eventually burned down and traces are now hard to find.

Unlike Mason and McReynolds, this is very much a forest lake. The road that leads there angles down the wooded hillside high above the lake, crosses the dam and then continues on around the other side just inside the trees toward an open area at the headwaters of Ruxton Creek. On the Pikes Peak Atlas this looks like a trail, but is a good road.

Though the forest is dense, all of the bank is walkable with no cliffs or scree slopes. (Fence-hoppers have been doing it in the dark for years, as the fishing litter shows). This is one of the most trespassed lakes in the area, for it is off by itself, has plenty of cover all around, and offers escape through rough country. It is simply a very long hike from anywhere, and only the most rugged

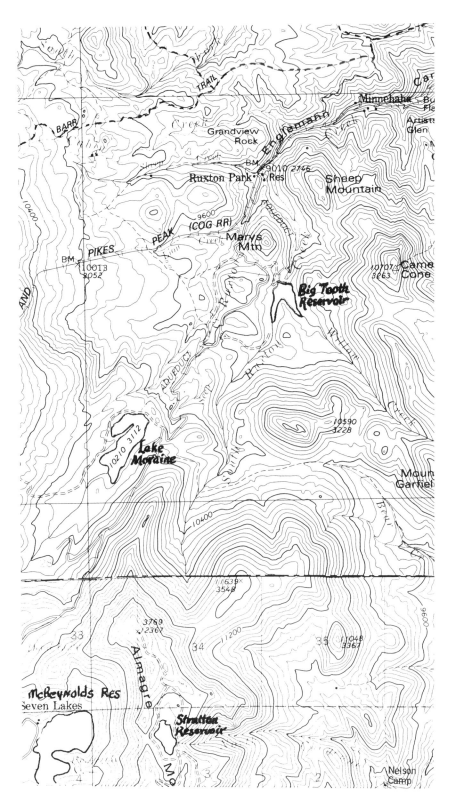

guerrillas try it because the closest legal camping is beyond the Cog Railway tracks along Sheep Creek off Barr Trail. **It is carefully watched, however, by the resident South Slope caretaker.**

Moraine is considered an excellent fish habitat and sports both cutthroat and brook trout of considerable size. Its fish population may be surveyed in 1992.

Moraine may grow someday. Engineers added 12 feet to the earthen dam a few years ago, hoping to recapture the capacity lost at Big Tooth, but the water level never changed! Ruxton Creek is aptly called Seep Creek where it emerges like a spring from beneath the dam and this leak kept the level from rising. Yet the seep may clog itself someday, making the level rise.

BIG TOOTH RESERVOIR #1, now 11 surface acres, deepest part now 41 ft., altitude 9,300 ft., built in 1924.

Big Tooth's dam has a bite out of it. Engineers declared the dam unsafe, and since repairs were considered too costly for its capacity, they carved a notch in the dam to drain most of it.

Now that it has been reduced to perhaps a third of its original size, there is still a rather large pool left with a self-sustaining brook trout population. Unnamed sources claim that trout grow to good size here. Big Tooth is the lowest lake on the South Slope, only 9,300 ft., so its reduced size and depth don't expose it to killer freezes.

But don't get the idea that Big Tooth is an abandoned lake off in the woods by itself. Water flowing through pipelines from higher lakes still makes a stopover at Big Tooth, so **it is constantly being checked on by the South Slope caretaker.**

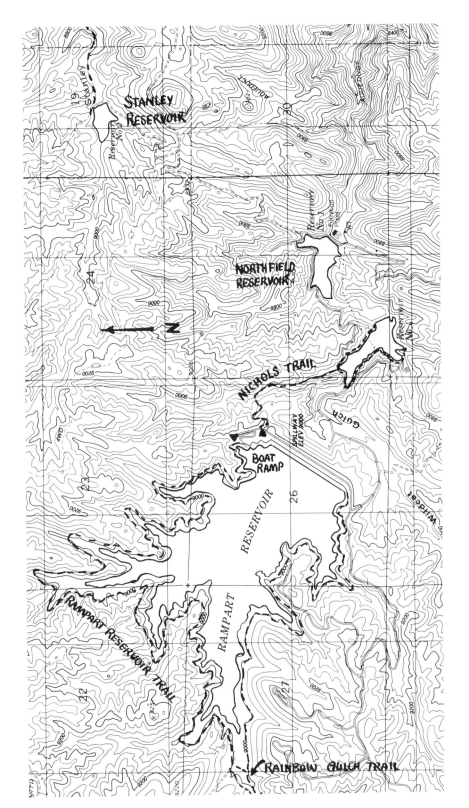

COLORADO SPRINGS NORTHFIELD (RAMPART) AREA

Northfield Reservoir (Closed)
Rampart Reservoir (Open)
Nichols Reservoir (Open)
Stanley Reservoir (Open to Some)

Mostly open to fishing, this popular area is a snapshot of how fishing rights develop in a drinking water system. The newest lake was built open (nobody seems to build closed reservoirs any more). One other has fishing rights leased to an organization, just as we find in other systems. **Only the oldest lake remains closed under the old rules—but that lake, too, may be opened!** This is the pattern that is repeated up and down Colorado's front range.

Northfield is the Water Department's name for this four-lake system that most people know as the Rampart Range area. And Northfield is also the name of the oldest lake in that system.

Most anglers are familiar with Rampart Reservoir, which is even open to gasoline-powered boating, and its baby cousin Nichols, a walk-in fishing lake just downstream. **Northfield is the next (and probably the next to be opened) jewel on that chain.** The fourth lake, Stanley, is off by itself to the north and is more familiar to hikers and mountain bikers because only the Air Force Academy is privileged to fish there.

It should be noted with gratitude that Rampart and Nichols were opened to fishing at the insistence of the Pike National Forest, which oversees all other kinds of recreation on those properties. When Rampart was proposed, the FS was simply unwilling to cooperate in the building of a closed reservoir on their property. Nichols was also opened as part of the Rampart deal.

ROAD DIRECTIONS: To find all but STANLEY, take the Rampart Range Road to Rampart Reservoir. You can access Rampart Range Road from the southern end of the Garden of the Gods in southwest

Colorado Springs or by taking Hwy. 24 from I-25 to Woodland Park, which involves less travel on gravel. The turnoff at Woodland Park is located next to McDonald, and the way is well marked. As you drive across the dam of RAMPART RESERVOIR, you can see Nichols down in the woods to your right. The large parking area at Dikeside Overlook serves both areas. The trailhead for Lake Shore Trail, which circles RAMPART, is near the boat ramp. The trailhead for NICHOLS is nearer the dam. When NORTHFIELD RESERVOIR opens, a gravel road between NICHOLS and NORTHFIELD will serve as a hiking trail to that lower lake.

To find STANLEY, take the south entrance to the Air Force Academy off I-25. Drive three miles, cross the railroad overpass and turn left onto Pine Drive. Go 5 miles. The paved road rises until you can see the Academy Hospital on your right. Look for a small gravel road on your left, immediately across from the hospital. This leads 0.9 miles back to the parking lot for Stanley Canyon Trail. There is limited parking, but more is available at the hospital.

NORTHFIELD RESERVOIR, 15 surface acres, deepest point 18 ft., altitude 8,680 ft.,built in 1890.

Hidden away in the woods below Nichols Reservoir lies what may be the next lake to be opened in the Colorado Springs water system. Northfield Reservoir has remained closed due to its position as settling pond for the old treatment plant located at its dam. However, that plant is due to be closed when a newer plant called McCullough is completed south of the Air Force Academy. This should allow Northfield to be opened for recreation, yet construction has yet to begin on the new plant, so it may be a few years.

Northfield could be a twin sister of Nichols upstream, for both are small forest lakes, but Northfield is shallower. Its banks are fairly gentle and easily accessible.

No fish surveys have yet been done, but Northfield is known to have a thriving brook trout population and probably has a few cutthroats and rainbows that escaped from Nichols.

Northfield has a full-time caretaker who lives next to the lake, so beware of jumping the gun on this lake's opening. If you want to hike in for a peek, first obtain a free permit.

RAMPART RESERVOIR, 519 surface acres, 11.6 miles of shoreline, deepest point 180 ft., altitude 9,000 ft., built in 1970.

Rampart is the most popular lake in the Colorado Springs system, open to boats and bait fishing, surrounded by a gently rolling trail that is open to horses and mountain bicycles. If you don't have a boat and want to fish remote arms of this large lake (highly recommended), bring your mountain bike. Just remember that the many inlets produce muddy sections during wet times.

Surrounded by evergreens, Rampart is most beautiful in early summer while Pikes Peak is still dressed in white. The Forest Service has built picnic areas overlooking the lake. **No camping is allowed at the lake itself, but you are allowed to fish all night, so long as you don't fall asleep.** Honest. I couldn't make up a rule like that, but I'm glad it exists. You may camp overnight at the Springdale Campground on Rampart Range Road, however. For reservations, call 1-800-283-2267. There is no potable water at the campground or at the lake.

Rampart's catch rate has improved due to the introduction of catchable sized Snake River cutthroats. It is also stocked with catchable rainbows and lake trout and has a few browns and brookies as well. **The special limit of one laker over 20 inches is vigorously enforced here because some anglers seem to be spoiling reproduction by taking smaller lakers, perhaps mistaking them for other kinds of trout.** Lakers are distinguished by the deep notch in their tail.

A 1990 creel survey showed that 89% of the fish taken were rainbows in the 8 to 14-inch range, followed by 10% lakers in the 12 to 19-inch range (return to water), 1% suckers and only 0.2 % brookies. But that was before the cutthroats were introduced to increase catch rates. The 1991 gill net census caught one brown measuring 18 inches, 21 lakers measuring 10 to 18 inches (too small to keep), three rainbows measuring 10-11 inches and four cutthroats measuring 11 to 12 inches.

The same sampling caught more suckers than anything else, but biologists are attacking that problem by stocking more lakers.

And by the way, lake trout do grow large, but they grow slowly. They live for 30 years and can give you many happy returns, so please consider releasing any laker—any laker—as an investment in future fun.

Gasoline-powered boats are welcome here. Rampart's boat ramp is very wide and presents no obstacles. Belly boats are also allowed. No swimming, wading, water skiing or other body contact is allowed. Dogs must be on a leash. No firearms, no fireworks, no open fires (grates only). The dam's access road is closed in winter, but cross-country skiers enjoy the lake shore trail via the Rainbow Gulch Trailhead on Rampart Range Road. However, **no ice fishing is allowed** because a winter drawdown often produces a dangerous hollow beneath the ice.

Bank fishermen will find most areas easily accessible, with few steep places. Shores are generally coarse sand with mud only at inlets. No large streams feed Rampart. Instead, its water comes via pipeline from beyond the Continental Divide.

NICHOLS RESERVOIR #4, 19 surface acres, deepest point 43 ft., altitude 8,720 ft.,built in 1913.

"Those Snake Rivers really like to bite and fight," says Forest Service Ranger Royce McCrary. "If you want cutthroats, try early in the morning or late in the afternoon with flies. They really like purple and yellow hair. The ones I tie look like a purple caterpillar."

Stocking catchable sized Snake River cutthroats along with the catchable rainbows has improved the catch rate at Nichols, now a very popular hike-in lake. "Bait is legal at Nichols and bait fishermen generally load up on rainbows," says DOW Biologist Douglas Krieger, "but cutthroat seem to prefer flies and lures."

Because they are stockers, most of the fish taken at Nichols are in the 10 to 12-inch range, but fish that escape early catching sometimes grow to 15 inches .

The hike to Nichols Reservoir only measures three quarters of a mile one way. It's uphill all the way back, but isn't very steep, climbing only 280 ft. It's a pretty trail, angling down through ponderosa pine, then following a drainage to the lake, where it forks to follow the shore in either direction. The trail now goes all the way around, except for the dam, which is closed to the public, so you do have to make a decision at that fork.

The shoreline trail stays about 30 feet above the water, following contours to stay fairly level. This is a National Forest trail, but the Youth Conservation Corps. did some of the work. The FS also takes care of litter barrels (but please pack it out instead of using them) and the restrooms. If you turn left at the fork, you'll find a double back-to-back vault restroom on the north shore. If you take the right fork, you'll find a single vault restroom located near the next creek inlet. There are none near the dam.

STANLEY RESERVOIR, 8.6 surface acres, deepest point about 30 ft., altitude 8,880 ft., built about 1911.

This beautiful lake is unique in the Colorado Springs system because Stanley has no other purpose than fishing. Colorado Springs owns the lake, but exclusive fishing rights have been leased to the U.S. Air Force Academy for many years.

The public is not banned from the lake itself, just from fishing there. The area is entirely open to hiking, mountain biking, horseback riding, even overnight camping more than 100 feet from the water. Fishing is allowed by special Academy permit only, but permit requirements have changed.

In the past, the permit system caused some ill will because **Colorado Springs residents, including retired military, could watch the Academy fish city-owned water but could not receive permits to fish that water themselves, even on a catch-and-release basis.** Now, however, a limited number of permits are reserved for retired military of any branch on a lottery basis. Numbers vary with fishing conditions, but generally about 150 out of 1,700 permits are sold to retired military who win the lottery. Preference points are awarded to lottery losers, so if you fail to win for three years in a row, you will surely win the fourth year.

Otherwise, special permits are sold only to Academy personnel and their bona fide house guests. The definition of a bona fide house guest is "a person who lives permanently outside of state and is actually staying in the home of Academy personnel." Since a valid Colorado fishing license is always required, house guests must have an out-of-state license.

The bag and possession limit is six trout of any size, only one of which can be over 14 inches. Bait fishing is permitted. Permits cost $7 per season or $3 per day.

The fishing lease arrangement goes way back. Originally, the city had a treatment plant that processed waters from both Stanley and West Monument Creek. Then Utilities moved the location of its plant to the mouth of West Monument Canyon.

This meant that Stanley's water no longer flowed naturally to the new plant. And since Stanley's flow is so small, it proved too expensive to pump it to the new location. Thus, it was no longer a source of drinking water for Colorado Springs or the Academy. Stanley became a fishing lake.

Just why the city didn't choose to open the lake to its own citizens can be understood in economic terms. Neither the Utility Dept. nor Parks and Rec. wanted to hired additional personnel to watch this one, small outlying lake, so it was cheaper to let the Academy manage recreation there. In return for fishing rights, the Academy from time to time grants to the city certain easements and rights of way at no charge.

The city has not abandoned the lake. The city continues to own the lake and property immediately surrounding it. The Academy's permit requirements are tight because all Academy waters receive about four times as much fishing pressure as the average Colorado lake, according to Bruce Rosenlund, U.S. Fish and Wildlife biologist. This is measured in fishing hours per acre per season, 2000 versus the state average of 500.

If you're not one of the lucky 150 retired military, Biologist Rosenlund suggests that anyone can catch identical fish at Fort Carson, where many hundreds of permits are available to the general public because there is twice as much water to fish and far less pressure.

Stanley's fish are paid for with permit fees—not taxpayer's money—and are purchased from the Leadville National Fish

Hatchery. The lake is stocked once a season with 600 eight-inch Snake River cutthroats. Most stockers are caught during the first season, but some join the resident population of reproducing cutthroats that grow to 15 inches.

COLORADO SPRINGS OUTLYING LAKES

Montgomery Reservoir (Open)
Homestake Reservoir (Open—See Aurora)
Upper Blue Reservoir (Open, But No Fish)

This section will concentrate on Montgomery and Homestake Reservoirs because Upper Blue has no fish. We count Upper Blue as "open" because you don't need permission to go there, but it will merit no more discussion here because it is drained every winter and there are no plans to attempt stocking.

MONTGOMERY RESERVOIR, 95 surface acres, deepest point 90 ft., altitude 10, 850 ft.,built in 1957.

ROAD DIRECTIONS: To Find MONTGOMERY from Denver, take I-70 west to the Frisco Exit, drive through Breckenridge and over Hoosier Pass. MONTGOMERY is visible on your right just as you start down from the top of the pass. You can see the access road on your right farther down.
From Colorado Springs, take Hwy. 24 west and turn right onto Hwy 9 just past Hartsel. When you meet Hwy. 285 below Fairplay, turn right on 285, then when you reach Fairplay, turn left to go through Fairplay, through Alma, and find MONTGOMERY on your left as you start to climb Hoosier Pass. The access road is good.

What used to be the old town of Montgomery now lies at the bottom of this high pass lake. The city acquired the land by buying up a lot of mining claims and they even had to move a ceme-

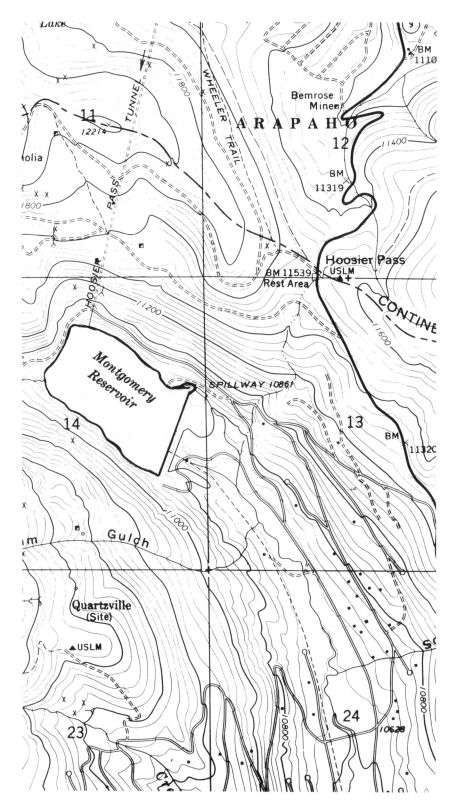

tery. Montgomery undergoes considerable draw-down each winter, so it will always be a marginal habitat and must depend upon put-and-take stocking, though some Pikes Peak cutthroat manage to breed in the stream above. There is no circling trail and the south side is nearly vertical, so fishermen hike the west and north sides. Do not fish from the dam.

The DOW stocks Montgomery with 24,000 catchable sized rainbows per season, so 85% of your catch will be rainbows. Some 20,000 Pikes Peak cutthroat fingerlings are also being tried.

No boating or floatation devices permitted, but the reservoir is open all night, when your chances are generally better. Ice fishing is banned because winter drawdown creates a cavity beneath the ice. The lake is open from May 1 to Dec. 1. Future improvements should include restrooms and trash barrels. There are none at the time of this writing.

HOMESTAKE RESERVOIR, 333 surface acres, deepest point 214 ft., altitude 10,260 ft., built 1967.

ROAD DIRECTIONS: To find HOMESTAKE from Denver, take I-70 west to Minturn and then Hwy. 24 south. Three miles south of Red Cliff, turn right onto Homestake road FS #703. To find the same turnoff from Colorado Springs, take Hwy 24 west through Leadville, over Tennessee Pass to the White River National forest. Look for Blodgett Campground on your left. That's Homestake road FS 703, leading up into the Holy Cross Wilderness. It's 11 miles to the Reservoir, but the last part is very rough and cannot be recommended for passenger cars. You need high ground clearance. At the base of the dam, the road forks to access both sides. The right fork is a little smoother than the left.

You're on top of the world at Homestake. Sharing its water with Aurora and Colorado Springs, Homestake Reservoir perches at the high snowy gates of the Holy Cross Wilderness Area. Lofty and cold, with fluctuating levels, it's a tough place for trout, and its rugged rocky banks make it a tough place for anglers, too, but despite all that, Homestake

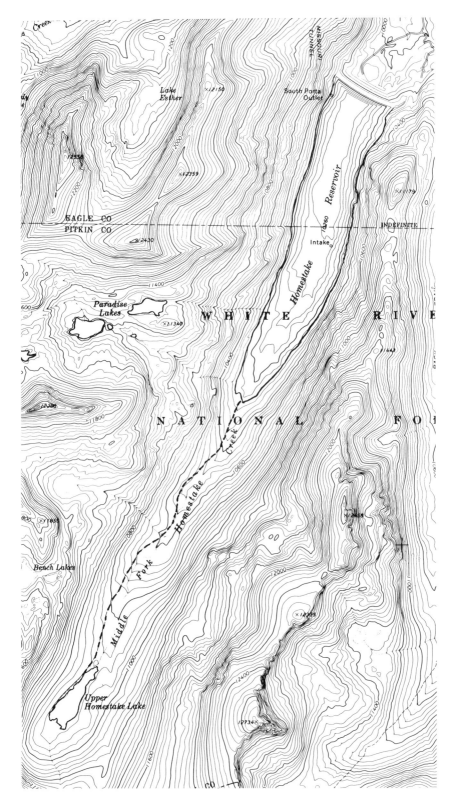

manages to get a lot of fishing pressure, even though many of its visitors are backpackers heading to even higher waters.

"We're stocking Colorado River cutthroat trout instead of rainbow now," says DOW Biologist Clee Sealing. "They're doing okay, but it's a tough spot. Fingerlings grow to about 10 or 11 inches. That's about all they can do before they get caught."

From the far end of the lake a creekside trail follows the Middle Fork of Homestake Creek to Upper Homestake Lake, a 17-acre baby sister that has bigger trout, cutthroat to about 13 inches. It's elevation is 10,500 ft.

Two miles up a steep trail that follows another drainage on the southwest edge of the main reservoir lies a group of timberline lakes known as Paradise Lakes. These four lakes are stocked with cutthroat also, but get heavy pressure from backpackers. Elevation: 11,200 ft.

Homestake itself is not within the wilderness area because the boundary runs just outside of it. Low-impact camping is allowed within the wilderness, but the best place is at the far end of the lake. Car-top boaters often take the left fork to Homestake because you can get to the water easier on that side. It's a rough road, and there is no boat ramp.

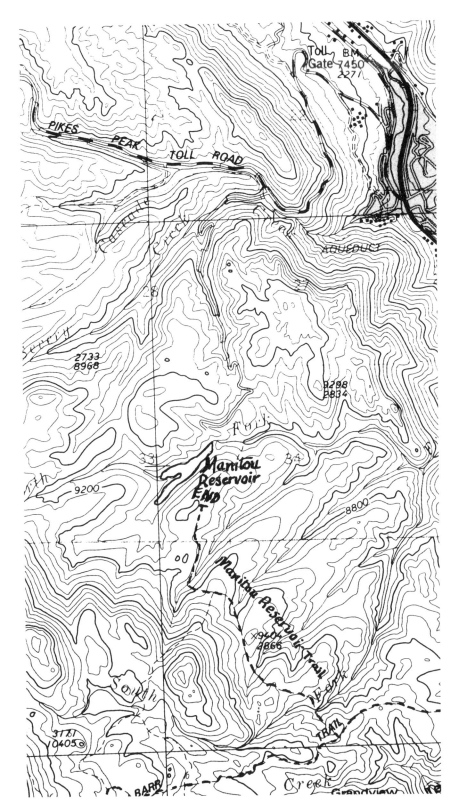

CITY OF MANITOU SPRINGS
1 Still Closed to All

Manitou Reservoir (Closed)

Stocked with sport trout, but closed to fishing? The one mountain lake serving Manitou Springs has caused a lot of talk and suspicion, but the city's story is almost as interesting as the rumors!

Tucked away in the woods on Pikes Peak, Manitou Reservoir (not to be confused with Manitou Lake near Woodland Park) is **closed to fishing but open to an unusual fish experiment.**

While other communities use copper sulfate to control algae in their reservoirs, Manitou is experimenting with a combination of fish in hopes of doing the same job naturally. "We haven't used copper sulfate in three years," says Water Dept. Chief Johnnie Price. "So far it seems to be working, and it's cheaper, too."

Copper sulfate is the same chemical used to keep algae from growing in waterbeds. It's an approved chemical, but the DOW hates it because it kills fish. Utility departments use it to prevent a scummy odor that is hard to remove once the water leaves the lake. This means treating the lake itself, fish and all.

In the old days, utility departments treated large areas of lake water with large doses and winced at the fish going belly up. Young fish seem to be hit the worst. Nowadays, departments use far less of the chemical and apply it in thin strips across the surface. The theory is that fish try to get away from it and have an easier time escaping if there is uncontaminated water on either side of the strip. But it still kills some fish.

"There has to be a better way," says Price. "Fish may have to be restocked now and then, but that's cheaper than buying chemicals."

So Manitou has stocked its lake at city expense with a non-reproducing variety of grass carp to eat moss, a few catfish to clean up the bottom and rainbows to eat other things. The rainbows are a Tasmanian strain, which isn't as exotic as it sounds, for it's a common strain used for sport fishing throughout the Rockies—and **that's why people talk. Who buys sport fish for a closed lake when the DOW would supply them free?**

The city insists that its lake is not open to any fishing at all by anybody. Period. When the city had a picnic at the lake, people were allowed to raft on the lake, but no fishing was allowed.

"I can't comment on what may or may not have happened years back," said Mayor Dan Wecks, "but current policy closes the lake to everyone." The primary reasons for closure are fire prevention and to protect fish that have been put there to control the algae problem.

If the city should someday consent to opening the lake to public fishing, perhaps even on a catch-and-release basis, the Division of Wildlife could provide rainbows free of charge, plus three-to-one matching funds for restrooms, trails, litter control and so forth. The division even has grass carp and catfish, though these fish are not generally stocked at such an altitude. (But that's what makes the experiment so unusual.)

MANITOU RESERVOIR, approximately 40 surface acres, deepest point 90 ft., altitude almost 9,000 ft., built in 1912 .

ROAD DIRECTIONS: If you're ever allowed to go there, the gravel road turnoff is located on the Pikes Peak Toll Road. Take the first left about 1.5 miles beyond the toll gate. It drops off sharply, so it's easy to miss. A locked gate on that road bars entry to the watershed.

A strange tunnel at Ghost Town Hollow runs ankle deep with spring water tapped from deep within Pikes Peak. Gold rush miners just couldn't believe that all of the area's gold was concentrated on the other side of the mountain at Cripple Creek and Victor, so they blasted a tunnel deep into the peak itself, hoping to find a mother lode.

The Cincinnati mine struck water instead of gold, but through the years that sweet water has proved more valuable than gold might have. For this strange spring provides much of the drinking water for a city famous for its other, more mineral-tasting springs.

From Ghost Town Hollow (named after the mining and lumber camp) the spring water forms the headwaters of North French

Creek and flows to Manitou Reservoir. This lake is deep because it's built in steep terrain, which also means that most of its shoreline is steep. There is no circling trail.

The closed watershed surrounding the lake is not fenced, so this is one place where innocent wanderers might wind up trespassing by mistake. Watch for signs. But even if vandals remove signs. being lost is not an acceptable excuse for trespassing. It is your responsibility to know where you are in these woods. **The penalty for trespassing here can be a fine up to $1,000 and/or 90 days in jail.**

Surrounded by evergreens, Manitou Reservoir makes a lovely scene as viewed from two popular hiking trails that branch off Barr Trail, which is the trail to the summit. One is called Manitou Reservoir Trail and legally dead-ends at an overlook of the lake. The trail doesn't actually dead-end. It legally dead-ends. As soon as you see the lake, that's where you have to turn around and back-track. There should be a sign to warn you, but again, sign or no sign, you must not trespass by approaching the lake.

Elk Park Trail actually crosses the northern edge of the watershed at Ghost Town Hollow, so no camping or horses are allowed in the North French Creek drainage. (You may camp in other drainages along this trail, however.) The city allows hikers and mountain bicyclists to cross the watershed by using this trail, but warns against exploring downstream, which immediately makes you a trespasser. For a complete description of these trails, including maps, see the *Trails Guide to Pikes Peak Country*.

With backpackers drooling at this lake in the distance, it is little wonder that Manitou Reservoir has been a popular target for moonlight poachers. But **the lake is very well guarded.** The caretaker's house is right on the lake, and he patrols with a trained security dog. What the caretaker may not see, the dog can smell.

Since Manitou buys its own fish, the DOW has no survey data. The only true wildlife fish are the naturally occurring brook trout, which probably attain good size here.

If you wish to hike the watershed, you must apply for special permission by contacting Johnnie Price at 685-5481.

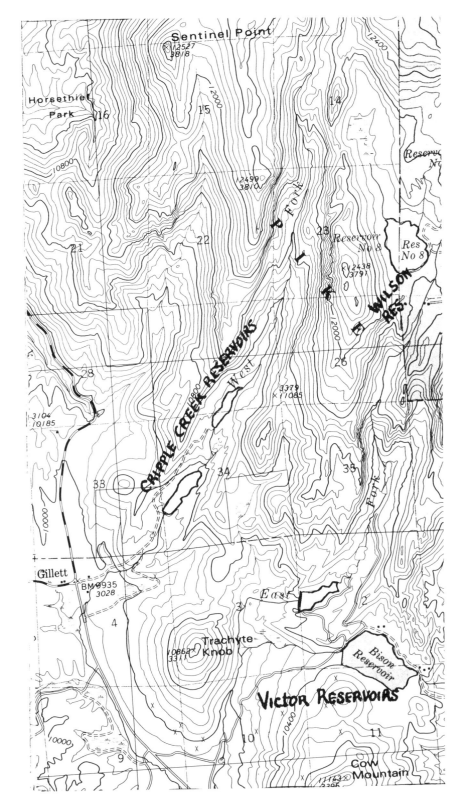

CRIPPLE CREEK LAKES
2 Lakes—Both Open To Some

Lower Cripple Creek Reservoir (No. 2)
Upper Cripple Creek Reservoir (No. 3)

Both of Cripple Creek's reservoirs are open to fishing on a restricted basis, but are closed to the general public. This historic town has found two unique ways to to safeguard its watershed: They lease the fishing rights to a club made up mostly of police and they allow the members to camp there overnight.

"We've never had to prosecute a trespasser," says Cripple Creek City Attorney Charlie Houghton. "Something about all those police officers camping there overnight just keeps trespassers away."

Cripple Creek doesn't have enough police to form a large club, so the membership of the Timberline Fishing Club has always been made up largely of Colorado Springs police. Most are retired now, but a few are still on active duty, according to spokesman Jerry Whiteman. The club's constitution requires that at least 10% (or 13) of its memberships go to ordinary Cripple Creek residents.

While open fires and overnight camping are forbidden on most mountain watersheds, Cripple Creek has used fire to fight fire. Campsites are situated away from trees, and campfires are restricted to established fire pits. Through the years, members have gathered and burned enough dead wood to keep their forest from becoming a firetrap, eliminating the costly and dangerous build-up of fuel wood so common in other watersheds.

Members do a lot of work on the watershed, improving drainage and roads. There is no trash and no place to put trash because members pack out every bit as they go. Members also provide portable toilets and pay to have them pumped out.

The club makes no profit, spending dues and guest fees on taking care of the watershed and on stocker rainbow trout purchased from a Boulder hatchery. Guests pay $5 each. Membership is limited and there is a waiting list, but members are allowed to sell their memberships directly, according to the city attorney.

In 1965 torrential rains burst both reservoir dams. Indeed, you can see the tail end of this destruction from Hwy. 67 at Gillett. Notice the notch in the wooded hillside to the east and the huge boulders scattered out on the plain below.

ROAD DIRECTIONS: The access road is closed to the public, but here's how guests can find it. Gillett is now just a bend in the highway on the way to Cripple Creek (13 miles from Divide and 5 miles from Cripple Creek). Take the gravel fork straight south from paved 67 at Gillett. Go south a quarter of a mile and find the turnoff on your left. Two locked gates guard the rough road to the watershed.

LOWER RESERVOIR #2, approximately 40 surface acres, deepest point 29 ft., rebuilt in 1966.

Stocked with rainbows, Lower Reservoir also has a few brookies. Browns stocked there years ago seem to be gone.

Lined with trees and rock outcroppings, this scenic lake has fairly accessible banks and a fisherman's trail along the shore. Members may even fish from the dam, but are not allowed to drive across it. Fishermen sometimes wade near the inlet.

UPPER RESERVOIR #3, approximately 30 surface acres, deepest point 19 ft., rebuilt in 1966.

Upper Reservoir was recently drained and may be drained again in 1992, so fishing here will have to wait for more stable conditions. This smaller and shallower lake has good potential, but it is a little harder to fish because the banks are steeper. However, there are beaver ponds with brook trout in the stream above the lake and even between the two lakes.

This area has abundant wildlife, including bear and bighorn, according to Chip Huffman of the Water Dept. Hikers wishing to explore the area—without fishing—may apply for a special permit by contacting City Attorney Charlie Houghton at 471-1212.

CITY OF VICTOR LAKES
One Open to Some
One Closed to All

Big Bison Reservoir
Little Bison Reservoir#2

The City of Victor has a mixed policy, one lake open to some Victor residents (but closed to the general public) and the other lake closed to everyone. For the past 30 years, exclusive fishing rights to the lower reservoir, Big Bison, have been leased to the Gold Camp Fishing Club for $1 a year. According to City Councilman and Club Spokesman Carl Roy, members must have a living dwelling in Victor, but the membership is absolutely closed, so no more Victor residents can join unless a member dies.

The upper reservoir is closed—even to club members—along with a couple of beaver ponds above the upper reservoir, all part of Victor's own property. But complicating matters is the public's right to fish other beaver ponds in the National Forest above Victor's property. For the first time, Victor has hired a full-time enforcement officer in addition to the live-in caretaker. The fine for trespassing alone is $300, and you can expect to be prosecuted to the fullest.

Trouble is, the city's own property is not fenced and water attorneys say that it has not been recently surveyed. Signs should warn away trespassers, but without a survey, it is hard to know how accurately these signs are placed. (More unfortunately, unpopular signs have a way of disappearing, and "I didn't see a sign" is not considered a good excuse in court.)

Many cities have agreements with the Forest Service, allowing them to lock people out of National Forest watersheds above the cities' own property, but Victor has no such agreement. **Thus,** the National Forest above Victor's property is open to public fishing, but you must be very careful. It is your responsibility to know where you are in the National Forest.

You have absolutely no right to reach these ponds by crossing private property (without permission) or Victor's property (permission unavailable). There is no trail and certainly no road access, but long-distance backpackers do manage to get there, generally by bushwhacking from the Bull Park area over Sheep Mountain. It's a very long and rugged journey, and the motive is generally adventure rather than fishing. To approach Bull Park, see our road directions to the Colorado Springs Seven Lakes area on the Pikes Peak South Slope.

But where is Victor's property? The beaver aren't talking and the Mayor refused us entry, so until we can mount an expedition, the true location of the legal ponds is in doubt. Beaver also move, so old maps are not reliable. Beaver ponds eventually fill up with silt, becoming a flat piece of grassland, while the beaver shift their operations either upstream or downstream. **Remember: It is your responsibility to know where you are when exploring Pikes Peak. Being lost is not an acceptable excuse in court.**

Imagine hiking along a stream in a long valley. Without some kind of accurate marker on the ground, how would you know exactly where you were, even with map in hand? Without personal knowledge, we have only one clue to pass along for what it's worth. Somewhere near the northern edge of Victor's property, there is an old earthen diversion dam for a reservoir that is no longer there. This does not mark the property boundary, mind you, but if you find any kind of man-made structure on that creek, you are probably trespassing and should high-tail it upstream as fast as you can.

City Attorney P.J. Anderson referred us to Attorney Ken Geddes, who referred us to Water Attorney Sandy MacDougall.

MacDougall was most helpful, showing us an official map, but since we have no personal knowledge, we cannot take responsibility for out-guessing the beaver. He also explained that there are old placer claims upstream, even though "there isn't a lick of gold." **MacDougall pointed out that your legal status on those** mining claims is possibly unlawful, though it is hard to say exactly where they are or if anyone really cares.

The Forest Service says that unpatented mining claims are no worry for backpacker anglers because those claims only convey mineral rights. The National Forest is pock-marked with old unpatented claims.

Patented claims, however, are like private property, so you would be trespassing there. MacDougall believes the claims in question are both patented and unpatented, so it will take some legal research to unscramble the mess.

Farther upstream, you reach the closed Colorado Springs South Slope watershed (Lakes Wilson and Bighorn), but the lakes there are drained each winter and have no fish. Hikers can get a free permit to go there, however. See our last chapter for instructions.

For a map of the area, see Cripple Creek.

ROAD DIRECTIONS: The road to Victor's watershed is closed to the public, but here's how guests can find it. From Divide on Hwy 24, take 67 south toward Cripple Creek for 13 miles. Gillett is just a bend in the road 5 miles from Cripple Creek. Take the gravel road due south from Gillett and drive two miles. The access road is on your left and is blocked by a locked gate.

BIG BISON, 20 surface acres, deepest point 15 ft., altitude 10,420 ft., completed in 1890.

"I think Big Bison is the most beautiful lake on Pikes Peak and I've seen them all, " Carl Roy told us. The lake is situated in a high bowl with gentle banks and views all around. The peak itself is visible from the eastern side of the lake, and from one point you can see the Sangre De Cristo Range. Large granite outcroppings similar to the Crags loom above the northeast shore. Bighorn sheep and deer frequent the area.

Non-member Victor residents can picnic at Big Bison free, but may not fish unless they are guests of a member and pay $5 each per day. The club makes no profit, spending dues and guest fees on paying the caretaker and buying stocker rainbows.

Club members do a lot of work at the watershed, improving

117

drainage and roads. There is no trash and no trash barrel because everyone packs out their trash as they go. Members are allowed to camp overnight.

Big Bison has not been used for drinking water in the past several years. A deal to sell its water to Cripple Creek fell through recently.

LITTLE BISON #2, 10-15 surface acres, deepest point 26 ft., altitude 10, 425 ft., complete 1897.

Little Bison is closed to fishing, but by all accounts fishing there is lousy anyway. Its water is more acidic than Big Bison, which means that it grows far fewer weeds and mosses, produces less fish food and, therefore, produces only very small brook trout. It is said to be a beautiful place, however, with a view of the peak.

GOT A LAKE-OPENER IN YOUR POCKET?

Why We Should Open Our Reservoirs

With tourists of the world flocking to Colorado to fish some of your drinking water, why shouldn't you be able to fish the rest? Why are so many of your reservoirs still closed?

After all, the same environmental studies and new thinking that led to opening some reservoirs may certainly apply to the rest. Public knowledge can only help to open more mountain lakes, so this chapter is aimed at giving you that knowledge. Without such knowledge, you're just a complainer.

The issue is far from settled, but times are changing, and so are the laws. This is an exciting time, an exciting opportunity, but what we don't need is a public rebellion to tear down the fences before preparations can be made.

That is the one thing that could really endanger what we all love. Prudent arrangements must be made to keep impact to a minimum. The watersheds need restrooms, trails, good access, adequate parking, litter control, fire control and law enforcement to safeguard our treasure. So a great deal more has to be done than just cutting a ribbon. Yet on the other side, those preparations should not take another century!

Your knowledge and interest and encouragement can go a long way toward giving your leaders the confidence they need to go ahead and get it done.

SO WHO'S TO BLAME?

There's a story about the Russian Revolution that illustrates our problem. When the Bolsheviks took over in 1917, they decided to take a fresh look at how the Czar had been stationing guards. They were mystified to discover that a guard had always stood alone in a certain spot in the middle of a palace lawn. There seemed to be no reason for it, so they dug through records to see how this strange posting had come about.

119

As it turned out, Catherine the Great had once strolled across that lawn and noticed a little flower blossoming there, a buttercup. Enchanted, the Empress called a guard and told him to make sure no one stepped on that buttercup. Of course, no one ever rescinded the order, so the flower bloomed and died of old age, but a guard continued to be stand watch on that spot—snow or shine—every day for more than a century!

Our watershed regulations are like that, dating back to the turn of the century. They just haven't been changed.

Guarding our reservoirs is a great responsibility, and our leaders have not taken this duty lightly. We all like clean drinking water. And whenever governments inherit a situation this old, prudence dictates careful review. There is a great temptation to leave things just as they are, especially when we are all pleased with the product rolling out of our faucets. Leaders want to be sure—and want to be reassured in every possible way—that any change won't be harmful.

Utility officials are engineers, not park rangers. They are proud to have built a system that works very well, 24 hours a day, so the idea of suddenly making changes smacks of fixing something that ain't broke. There is a natural reluctance to have the public underfoot. For generations, that reluctance has been very firm in many communities, but times are changing.

One nagging problem is the question of who will manage recreation on utility lands. Water departments are not park and recreation departments. They don't want to be in that business. They are correct in pointing out that the state and cities already have departments to do park and recreation work, yet these are generally overwhelmed and underfunded. It will take creative approaches to find the cheapest ways to manage new recreation, perhaps requiring user fees, donations or volunteer help.

Meanwhile, utility departments are often the only presence at these remote areas miles from the nearest city park. We need to encourage park and recreation departments to examine priorities and get involved on city lands far from the city limits.

Most of all, we should thank our present officials for doing something that nobody else ever did, instead of grumbling that it should've happened sooner. If your city's bandwagon is rolling now, it might do more good to cheer and help to pull it. If your city's bandwagon is stuck in the mud, talk to your neighbors and phone your mayor.

HOW DID WE GET INTO THIS MESS?

Imagine an era when no one treated sewage or drinking water—and when people dug wells and outhouses in their own yards. People got pretty nervous—and sometimes sick—so when growing communities started piping water from the mountains, it only seemed reasonable to keep people from making a mess of that water.

Around the turn of the century, the federal government began making agreements with local communities, setting aside large areas of National Forest as watershed and parceling out land grants to cities. The details put most people to sleep, but there are several points that every citizen should know:

—**Cities were given deeds.** Cities own most of these lakes, not the federal government. The maps are now crazy quilts of federal and city-owned lands. Part of a watershed may still be federal, but often the lake itself and its shores are city-owned and city-controlled. **It is public property, but if you are not a citizen of that city, you have no vote. Still, you do have an interest! If you open your reservoirs to citizens from another town, it's only fair that they open their reservoirs to you.**

—Your U.S. Forest Service is definitely pro-recreation and is not in the business of keeping people out of the National Forest. Closure runs counter to their philosophy. It was all done to safeguard communities before the dawn of modern water treatment.

—It shouldn't take a plane-load of lawyers flying to Washington to renegotiate these old agreements. That work generally can be done locally.

—The agreements never actually banned fishing by name, just human activity (and grazing and mining). **The ban on fishing is a local policy, not a federal one.**

—The primary purpose of any reservoir is drinking water, not recreation. If engineers need to drain a lake to make repairs, fishermen can't complain. Recreation must always take a back seat, but **it so happens that environmental conditions that produce good fishing also produce good water quality.**

That last point is vitally important because game fish are sensitive pollution-testers. They're like the canaries that coal miners used to detect dangerous shifts in the environment. When the canaries stopped singing, miners knew they were in trouble and ran to report it. And when game fish go belly up in our drinking water, the public is in trouble and should run to report it.

Sport fish watch the water, and sportsmen watch the fish. But that presupposes that sportsmen are allowed to watch the fish. Shutting out the watchmen is no way to instill public confidence.

CAN WE GET PERMISSION TO SEE THESE FORBIDDEN AREAS?

Generally speaking, yes, except in places like Boulder or perhaps Victor. Special permits are free and fairly easy to obtain from most cities, although very few people ever go to the bother. But it generally takes more than a phone call!

In Colorado Springs, for example, you must get an appointment with Don Mulligan, manager of water operations. Go to his office, show him where you want to go, exactly when and why and what you want to do there. "We try to be very accommodating," says Mulligan, "but we want a chance to look you in the eye and explain the rules and why those rules exist."

Your permit will be a letter typed by Mulligan's secretary and signed by him. You receive one copy and another copy is sent to the caretaker by mail, so **you can't get a permit on short notice. You need to arrange this about a week in advance**. The caretaker will then be expecting you on a certain date at a certain time and will make sure that you obey the rules and leave on time (before dark). In other words, while you watch birds with binoculars, the caretaker might be watching you with binoculars.

Other cities may require even more. Cripple Creek, for example, wants you to sign a waiver and show proof of insurance. Boulder is the one community that absolutely bans all but essential personnel. Even the city attorney says he has never seen the place!

BUT WHY DON'T THEY GIVE SPECIAL PERMITS FOR FISHING?

Good question. Most cities will grant special permission to hike or picnic or to watch birds or wildlife in a closed watershed, and that's why officials often object to calling them "closed."

Most watersheds are technically "open by special permit." But you cannot get a permit to fish!

Doesn't this discriminate against fishermen? Well, yes. And aren't hiking and bird-watching human activities just like fishing? Yes. And don't hikers and bird-watchers have to go to the bathroom just like fishermen?

Well, *I've* never worn a diaper when hiking a watershed!

So what's so dirty about fishing? **Most utilities officials agree that dragging a lure across a lake does not affect water quality, and certainly fishermen are no more dirty than birdwatchers. But there are a lot more fishermen than birdwatchers!**

If only hiking and bird-watching were allowed, even our most popular lakes might become very lonely places and area tourism would definitely suffer. Special permits are not available for fishing forbidden lakes because too many people would want them.

So if zillions of people applied for special permits to hike, picnic or to watch birds or wildlife in watersheds, you can bet that special permits would dry up. For practical reasons, you are only welcome if practically nobody wants to go.

Since tourism is a vital part of the state economy, it might make sense—even dollars and sense—to trade "No Trespassing" signs for "Welcome" signs.

BUT SHOULDN'T OUR DRINKING WATER RESERVOIRS BE CLOSED TO FISHING?

Not unless you want to ban fresh-water fishing throughout America. Because when you get right down to it, just about all fresh water is somebody's drinking water. Follow it downstream, and you'll find an intake.

When tourists stand atop Pikes Peak or ride the Cog Railway and admire the mountain's jewels, they laugh out loud or express outrage when told that certain lakes are off-limits because they are drinking water reservoirs. Tourists have that reaction because— back home—they grew up fishing and recreating on their own drinking water reservoirs. They talk about making good drinking water out of the next city's treated sewage because that's how much of America makes drinking water, period. To hear them talk, we are foolish for not making use of our resources in a modern way. And they resent it, too. They came all this way, and somebody yanked away their "Welcome" sign.

WHAT HAPPENED TO THE GOOD OLD DAYS WHEN PEOPLE COULD DRINK NATURALLY PURE WATER?

Andrew Jackson probably fought his most famous battles with his pants down because he had raging diarrhea that wouldn't go away. It broke his health, turning him into the haggard old man we see on the $20 bill. Andy caught it during the Creek War just before marching to New Orleans and he had cramps so bad that he used to hang himself over bent saplings, trying to use that pressure to ease his belly. His secretary wrote that Jackson sometimes couldn't eat and lived off weak gin and water.

There's your clue. Tough Old Hickory probably became infested with parasites.

Throughout history, various kinds of water-borne disease have been common among armies because so many people camping together tend to pollute the camp's water supply. The same goes for villages and cities wherever sewage and water supplies aren't well treated. Even if people are as tough as Old Hickory, some get sick and some don't, some get well and some don't, some die and some don't, and some just stay sick for the rest of their lives. It has always been like that. That's the real history.

No matter what they taught you in school, no matter what you have seen or read or heard, there has never been pure drinking water on the surface of this planet. Under the surface, sure. There are fountains of pure drinking water from beneath the surface, but that cold sparkling stream tumbling from a glacier-fed lake far from any human impact can make you real sick unless you treat it just right. Because pure surface water is a thing of myth and legend, not a scientific reality. Natural germs were polluting surface water before human beings ever evolved.

And nobody is more disappointed than I am because I used to associate a cold drink from a stream with really getting away from it all, getting back to nature, back to purity.

It just wasn't true.

No army has to be camping upstream. No careless fisherman or camper is necessarily at fault, because the big concern among healthcare professionals in this area is a single-celled parasite called giardia that is spread by beaver and deer, by bats and birds, by creatures both warm-blooded and cold-blooded. **Giardia has** even been found in bony fish, so if the fish have it, you can stop blaming the fisherman.

Giardia never swims outside of an intestine, but if a critter has an intestine, it can have giardia. In bustling Bangladesh or Bangkok, people might be the critters at fault, but only because people are the most common critters in those parts. **Hiking deep into the woods to escape human impact will not help you escape giardia, because it is spread by all kinds of wildlife worldwide, spread to the most remote streams and spring pools. Including the pristine waters of Colorado, open or closed.**

Yes, a tumbling stream stirs oxygen into the water, which burns up bacteria, but that doesn't do anything to the tough egg-like cysts that spread giardia. In fact, the cold temperatures of our mountain water even work to preserve giardia cysts, making them harder to kill with treatment pills in your canteen. That is not what I was taught in junior high science, but that is what I learned the hard way:

We were camped at one of the greatest little fishing spots in the Pike National Forest, a remote hike-in place where the rangers themselves generally take their limit of fine brookies. But there I came down with a double attack of vomiting and diarrhea.

I had experienced milder attacks before, diarrhea and cramps mostly, but they had always gone away quickly, and that turns out to be common with giardia. It fools you by seeming to go away, then comes back stronger later. This time my wife had to help me out of the woods, and that was enough to send me to a doctor.

"We'll run some tests to make sure, but I think I know what's wrong," said Dr. Bildstein. "You're infested with parasites. Have you been up in the mountains at all?"

I remember being more horrified than embarrassed. Sure, the so-called expert guide-author was going to have a tough time living down a third water-borne disease, having already graduated from brutal gastroenteritis and jungle amoebic parasites in other parts of this continent. But I was more horrified that, once again, I was being eaten up from the inside by a gut full of crocodiles.

And I thought I had been so careful! All those smelly, nasty-tasting chlorine and iodine tablets that I had pinched into canteens. And I still got giardia! It was enough to make a man turn to gin without the water.

Fortunately, we now have drugs like Flagyl that can treat and cure giardia, but not before I lost a lot of weight.

That's when it hit me: Instead of worrying that people might spread disease on a mountain watershed, we need to worry about the opposite. You might catch giardia from nature's watershed.

Don't get giardia. Take water from home on day trips. Just freeze about a third of a canteen-full overnight and top it off next morning with good city tapwater and a dash of generic sparkling water. It'll stay cold all day and you'd swear you filled it from a stream. For longer trips, take a pot and boil water for several minutes—a real rolling boil—then cool it and put it into a canteen and chill that in a stream. When it gets cold, you'll love it.

Filtration systems sold in fishing and mountaineering shops work, but they have a flow-rate problem—too much work for too little water. Treatment pills work, but only if you use them **exactly** as directed.

That's how I got in trouble. If one tablet can theoretically make muddy water drinkable, it seemed to me that less chemical would be enough to treat the sparkling clear stuff that trout and I love. But that's wrong. Giardia is so tough to kill chemically that it requires the full dose and the full waiting time at the proper temperature (prewarming is best), and even then, researchers have been astonished at how hard it is to kill giardia. **That's why I prefer boiling. Boiled water tastes better and besides, giardia deserve boiling!**

Oh, I know. You've been drinking raw stream water for years and have never had a problem, so your favorite stream must be okay, right?

Wrong. Because giardia is spread by cysts from feces—any kind of feces—which means that cysts come and go as the stream flows. One canteen-full may be free of them and the next canteen-full may be contaminated. You can't tell.

And then there is the little matter of individual resistance. Many people seem to have the ability to keep giardia from growing into a problem. The parasite simply takes up residence, but doesn't build an overwhelming population. That person then becomes a carrier, personally immune but able to pass on the disease to others. But sometimes even such resistant folks get a dose big enough to cause a problem, so don't listen to people who assure you that they've never gotten sick. You still might get sick or they might get sick next time, if they get a stronger dose.

Another thing. Spring water should be pure as it comes from

underground, but **springs generally ooze into pools that are open to contamination by feces from mice or birds or whatever.** "I won't drink it unless I can catch it flowing straight out of a rock," says Dr. Frank Barry, a Colorado Springs sports medicine specialist.

All in all, keeping people away from a watershed doesn't really protect the water against giardia because giardia is simply part of the ecology, part of the landscape. If you go there, remember: **Treat your water.**

UGH, BUT DON'T WE HAVE MODERN TREATMENT PLANTS?

Yes. And that is a big change! NOWADAYS, ALL OF THE CLOSED WATER IN THIS BOOK FLOWS TO MODERN WATER TREATMENT PLANTS. THE STATE HEALTH DEPT. SAYS THAT NO NEW TREATMENT PLANTS HAVE TO BE BUILT TO ACCOMMODATE RECREATION ON THE FRONT RANGE.

The 1992 opening of the North Slope lakes on Pikes Peak was delayed until Cascade received tapwater that is filtered as well as chlorinated. That didn't happen until Colorado Springs provided the water. Ironically enough, once that hook-up was made, Cascade had better water—at least, more thoroughly treated water—than the most fashionable area of Colorado Springs.

You might think that the wealthiest homes would have dibs on water from the city's finest treatment facilities, but not so. The Broadmoor area, including my own home, is part of the old South Suburban Water District that never had a filtration plant. It's pretty good water, even if it isn't legal under the newest guidelines now going effect, but **it does not flow from a closed watershed** and this has caused some confusion.

Imagine water flowing down from motorcycle country, through National Forest where people hike and camp overnight and ride horses and mountain bikes, down past the beer-party rendezvous on Gold Camp Road, down Helen Hunt Falls with all its tourists, down through city picnic grounds to the intake in Cheyenne Canyon, with only one restroom enroute.

This is more human impact, more kinds of recreational impact than anyone ever proposed for any of the closed watersheds, but this water flows from an open watershed and has never been filtered—only very carefully chlorinated.

Since water from the same city's closed watersheds IS filtered, many fishermen find this whole situation very odd to say the least. Closed watersheds have modern water treatment, but open watersheds don't?

How do people avoid getting giardia from this water? Since my wife and I have been drinking this same tapwater at our own home for the past 17 years, I've looked into this thoroughly.

It seems that chlorination—expertly done—should kill giardia, but only if there are never any slip-ups. It's a 24-hour job. Tiny communities have trouble because the poor fellow in charge of chlorination generally had a lot of other jobs to do, so slip-ups tended to be more common. Colorado Springs, on the other hand, has a highly professional staff hired to watch things constantly. In other words, Colorado Springs personnel been very very careful!

Needless to say, the city is scrambling to build a new plant to complete their system, but irregularities in site selection and lack of public consultation has resulted in uproar and delays that may lead to a better site being used. It might also lead to some hefty fines because the Environmental Protection Agency has a deadline and is getting ready to ride Colorado Springs like a jockey with a whip and spurs.

So far as health authorities are concerned, there is only one way good enough to guard against problems like giardia. We must treat all of the water all of the time in a way that eliminates all problems, even if a little slip-up occurs. That means back-up.

Giardia is so hard to kill with chemicals that **the Health Dept. requires both filtration and chlorination.** Actually, it's a multiple back-up system: chlorination, then coagulants to make particles stick together, then filtration to remove all that, followed by still another chlorination. Do all that and no midnight slip-up can do much harm.

And that is how water is already treated from closed watersheds on the front range.

But for those still worried about the impact of fishing on water supplies, there is a huge surprise.

FISHING IMPROVES WATER QUALITY?

Yes, fishing improves water quality. Fishing makes a lake so much cleaner that laboratories can document the change.

In Montana, authorities studied a remote lake that was opened to fishing after being closed for many years. They kept track of the amount of fecal bacteria in the water before and after opening. Rain always made the levels go up because rain washes feces into the lake. But **after opening the lake to fishing, bacteria levels went down and stayed down, rain or shine.**

The reason is wildlife. A closed reservoir is a magnate for large animals that poop on the shore and in the water. When fishermen show up, animals move back into the woods and drink from streams higher up. They may return at night, but the end result is less total poop on the shore and less fecal bacteria in the water.

Back in 1913, this situation didn't exist because there was so little wildlife. Elk were almost extinct in Colorado, and in 1910 a census found only 5,000 deer in the entire state. Now Colorado boasts 750,000 deer and 170,000 elk, more elk than any other state. Most other kinds of wildlife have boomed as well.

When it comes right down to it, all God's critters gotta poop, but only man cares where. People do use the restrooms provided, more so when they are clean restrooms. But even when anglers find themselves too far away from the restroom, they generally walk uphill, scrape out a hole with the heel of a boot and do their business in the environmentally correct way. No other animal cares. **So isn't it odd that we ban people?**

In 1981, our Pikes Peak Committee for Freer Use of Public Lands presented the Montana study to Colorado Springs Utilities. The department was surprised, to say the least, and just a little suspicious, because they were armed with some creepy studies showing that germs increase if a lake is opened to such things as swimming and waterskiing. (This is true because toilet paper simply doesn't do the whole job, so you can actually measure fecal bacteria increasing when swimmers start soaking Remember that when your dog gets off the leash and plunges into your reservoir!)

Yet Colorado Springs has a lab of its own and reservoirs both open and closed, so they checked it out for themselves. By the time the North Slope Watershed Advisory Committee was meeting **11 years later, the Utilities' own lab had figures showing that South Catamount Reservoir—while closed—consistently had far more fecal germs than Rampart Reservoir, which has always been open! Indeed, Rampart generally tests zero.**

To be fair, we should mention a study done in Springfield, Mass., which showed a somewhat opposite effect, but that is not surprising when you consider that Springfield, Mass., simply doesn't have the elk, deer and other concentrations of wildlife found in Montana and Colorado.

And what does the Colorado Health Dept. say? A member of the North Slope Watershed Advisory Committee contacted Jon Scherschligt, Chief of the Ground Water and Standards Unit, Water Quality Control Division of the Colorado Health Dept. Here are excerpts from his written reply, dated August 8, 1991: **"We have never to my knowledge been confronted with any situation in Colorado where fishing has been shown to cause any measurable walter quality damage. . . The Water Quality Control Division feels that the use of a water supply reservoir for fishing does not in and of itself pose any threat to water quality.**

In fact, the same letter put the shoe on the other foot. While utility departments might worry about fishing, the Health Dept. worries about utility departments themselves causing significant pollution by releasing sewage that is not treated well enough.

All this this makes sense, when you think about it, but people aren't used to thinking about this kind of thing. We react in old ways. We are used to hearing about human pollution, man-made problems, human-to-human disease. We tend to forget the actual reality—that nature isn't pure, that we are all animals (some more careful than others), that wildlife drops feces wherever, that wildlife can give us disease. In a real world situation, Tarzan might easily catch parasites and wither away to look like Peewee Herman!

BUT WON'T FISHING HAVE IMPACT ON WILDLIFE AND PRISTINE WILDERNESS?

"Sorry, Mr. Fisherman. We can't let you into our closed watershed because it's an untouched, pristine nature preserve. There has to be some place on earth set aside, locked away safe from all human impact. And besides, today we're dynamiting."

Watersheds are not wildlife refuges. If they were, you could fish there automatically, because wildlife refuges are open to fishing! Because fishing is a low-impact use.

Watersheds are not wilderness areas. If they were, you

could fish there automatically, because wilderness areas are open to fishing! Because fishing is a low-impact use.

Watersheds are actually remote industrial parks that happen to have some wildlife and wilderness, but their major function is the production of water, not the protection of nature. In other words, a water department has to bulldoze trees, dig trenches, blast rocks, lay pipelines, erect power lines, operate trucks and graders, pour concrete, doing lots of high-impact industrial stuff that might shock armchair environmentalists who always thought of their watersheds as pristine, untouched nature preserves. Nature does do well on our watersheds (except Boulder's), but all this high-impact industrial activity simply can't compare to the low-impact caused by fishermen walking in and casting a lure.

Of course, water departments don't have complete freedom to bulldoze the environment. A threatened & endangered butterfly can stop everything, even on land owned by the water department. They are constantly hassling with federal permits, for example, if the land is federal. In most cases, they do a good job of cleaning up after their work, just as a thoughtful backpacker cleans up a campsite and tries to make it look natural again. They aren't out to butcher the environment, but nature preservation is not their main mission, either.

The nature preserve argument is one of the strangest excuses ever offered to keep anglers out of a watershed. It works to enlist the support of us environmentally minded folks who are sick of seeing nice places trashed, but if watersheds were untouched, we would all be drinking from backyard wells because it does take some equipment to maintain reservoirs and their plumbing.

In a real wilderness area, even the Forest Service cannot use a chain saw to cut a downed tree: They have to use a hand saw. And if they want to go somewhere, they have to walk or ride a horse. They can't even use a mountain bicycle.

Imagine trying to run a watershed that way. Boulder's Skyscraper Reservoir is now part of a wilderness area, and that has turned the tables. The public can fish at Skyscraper, but the city cannot use equipment there. Fortunately, Skyscraper doesn't need much attention because its water simply flows downstream to Barker.

Of course, we do need to preserve nature. That's why thoughtful citizens don't lobby to throw open watersheds suddenly, without plans and preparations that take the environment into account. For example, parking lots at the North Slope on Pikes

Peak were selected to take advantage of old gravel pits and a meadow so a lot of trees didn't have to be murdered to make way for parking.

Yes, the public wants to have its cake and eat it, too, wants to preserve nature's beauty while still enjoying careful, limited access. But for real sportsmen, that is the beauty and the joy of the sport. The two really do go together. If I had to wreck a place in order to fish it, I'd rather stay home.

WHAT ABOUT FIRE DANGER?

Lots of mountain lakes have trees around them, precious trees that no one wants to see burn, yet trees don't disqualify lakes from being used for fishing. Nevertheless, fire is a watershed manager's nightmare, so fire is often a big issue.

When Nature's cycles are working correctly, forest fires do good as well as harm. Small fires clear out dead wood, returning nutrients to soil, making grassy parks with more to eat for wildlife. And best of all, small fires prevent big fires.

The first trees to grow up after a fire are the aspen, which provide the shade that tiny conifers need to get started. Eventually conifers grow up through the aspen, replacing them until you have a climax forest of solid conifers (and little to eat for wildlife). This sets the stage for a fire that will open up clearings for aspen, starting the whole cycle over again. And while that cycle is at work, aspen serve as firebreaks. Green aspen don't burn well, so an aspen grove can actually stop a fire's progress.

The real trouble begins with a run of good luck. If no fires happen, the climax forest gets old and choked with dead wood, creating a fuel pile that cannot burn small. Such a firetrap can create a blaze so hot that trees die to the root, letting soil wash away to fill up lakes with mud, turning lakes to swamp and leaving the soil-damaged hillsides unable to grow more trees.

You can see a place like that in the Lost Creek Wilderness. Lake Park has no lakes, just bogs, and the surrounding ghost forest looks like ocean driftwood almost a century after the fire (*Trails Guide to Pikes Peak Country*, pg. 203).

Fear of fire is one reason why watershed managers have long tried to keep people out, but this policy—along with a century of good luck—has worked to create firetraps in some our most precious areas. All remedies seem risky. One sure way to pick an area clean of firewood is to allow people to camp there, as Cripple Creek and Victor do. You know how impossible it can be to find firewood in the average campground. Yet campers might also start a fire in such a firetrap. The same goes for a wood-cutter's carnival.

What can be done when "No Trespassing" produces a firetrap? For example, Colorado Springs has always had a little-known policy of issuing permits to cut firewood in the watersheds, but officials have been reluctant to publicize this policy because they didn't want a stampede. This low-key approach backfired in a public relations sense: People who noticed the wood-hauling grumbled bitterly that only insiders were cutting wood.

And that's not true.

To obtain a free permit to cut wood on Colorado Springs watersheds, call Don Mulligan at 636-5616 and make an appointment. Your permit will be specific for a certain location. You will agree on a date and time so the caretaker can meet you and open gates. Only one permit per day per watershed is granted. Commercial operators are not welcome. Most roadside and easily-accessed areas have been picked clean by now, so be prepared to drag wood from deeper in the timber. You are not allowed to drive off the roadways.

When our citizens committee began mediation with Colorado Springs a dozen years ago, fire plans were a major source of unhappiness among various governments involved. Brainstorming resulted in some new perspectives:

—**Keeping people out will not prevent fire.** Half of all wildfires in Colorado forests are caused by lighting, so even if no one ever goes into the woods, lighting will someday set fire to our watersheds. We must plan for this eventuality.

—**Keeping people out may contribute to a firetrap**, so more wood must be removed in a controlled manner.

—**Keeping the public out doesn't keep people out, for trespassers and city personnel use the watershed unobserved.** While hiking watershed roads under special permit, I found many cigarette butts apparently thrown from city vehicles. Public scrutiny can help prevent such abuse.

—**Since it is too late for natural fires to benefit the watershed, artificial areas must be created to simulate small-fire clearings.** State foresters helped prepare the North Slope of Pikes Peak in just this way, strategically clearing small areas and allowing aspen to grow as fire breaks.

—A forest fire demands total cooperation among governments without buck-passing or squabbles over boundaries. Even the Army should be enlisted because they have equipment and manpower already paid for. Colorado Springs now has its own wild fire unit, and **agreements have been made which allow various governments to fight fires with no worries about boundaries for the first four hours.**

—All personnel should have fire-fighting and communications gear on hand, even if fire fighting is not their usual job.

—Removing dead wood also removes valuable nutrients from the forest (unlike fires that return nutrients) and wood-burning produces pollution, so a better remedy may lie in using a heavy-duty chipper to grind up wood and leave it to rot where it grew.

BUT WON'T PEOPLE TRASH OUT OUR WATERSHEDS?

"Fishermen would trash the place!" is a claim we heard over and over from managers of closed watersheds. Like it or not, that's the impression they have.

And they're not entirely wrong, are they?

Water managers are not park managers. They're not used to picking up after people. **Never mind that nobody closes city parks because of litter. In a watershed, litter can change everything.**

Soon after the opening of Penrose-Rosemont, somebody made a big mess there. According to the lease, the DOW had the job of cleaning up litter, but of course they never planned to be there every day, so the mess sat awhile. The caretaker was understandably enraged, took pictures and presented them to the DOW. Their hair stood on end, and officers hurried to clean it up, but this started a rumor in Colorado Springs that the lake was being reclosed because it was "trashed out."

The fact that the lake was drained dry for repairs didn't stop the rumor. The rumor got around and it worked to persuade some people that opening more lakes would be a bad idea.

Just one batch of litter, maybe not even left there by fishermen, did damage far beyond the temporary eyesore it created.

Actually, a few beer cans at water's edge don't really damage water quality from a laboratory point of view, but that's not the point. **Trash is more than a mess. It's a red-letter sign saying** that somebody doesn't give a damn about the planet, its beauty, and everything that so many of us hold precious. It's a message so loud and clear that it can be heard echoing miles away and for years after the mess is cleaned up!

That's why packing out your own trash is not enough. You need to make sure others do the same—and clean up after them if they don't. They might get the hint, and even if they're not around, the place will be cleaner for your efforts. It isn't a futile gesture. It really works for a reason that few people consider:

How do you behave at a garbage dump? Even the most considerate person sees nothing wrong with dumping garbage in a garbage dump. So when people visit a trashed out site, they tend to drop more. But when they find a place clean, they tend to have the opposite reaction. On average, it simply works out that people who follow you will behave differently if they find no trash there. Picking up litter actually helps to prevent more litter. At least, on average.

Just about the cleanest trail in the Pike National Forest is one that only fly fishermen frequent. It's called Gill Trail along the Gold Medal waters below Denver's Cheesman Dam. Recently, I had the honor of carrying out the only piece of litter I found all day, which left it spotless. I like to think someone dropped it by mistake.

Yet I wish I could say the same for some of the places where bait fishermen go. Certainly I have nothing against bait fishing. Most of us started out by dunking a worm and some of us still do. But if you like to fish with bait—and half of Colorado anglers do—then please understand that **bait fishermen need to clean up their act.** I've seen places where most of the litter was discarded bait containers!

The DOW never, never, never makes rules against bait fishing just to keep down litter, but you should know that certain watershed managers do have this in mind. When discussing how to protect a beautiful and sensitive area, banning bait fishing is often tops on their list.

One form of littering that some anglers think is "natural" is the habit of throwing fish cleanings into the water. During snagging season at Elevenmile, it can be hard to wade near the main boat ramp area without stepping on salmon heads. Colorado's cold water tends to preserve such garbage, so even though rotting fish occur in nature, remember that nature does some nasty things sometimes. **Biologists beg you not to throw cleanings into the water!**

And by the way, the Penrose-Rosemont story had a happy twist. After resolving that one incident, utility officials kept a close eye. Years later, officials told me that they were actually surprised at how little problem they experienced on average there. They were eventually impressed and quite pleased with the way anglers behaved at this experimental lake, and that smoothed the way for opening more!

SURELY SOMEBODY IS FISHING THESE CLOSED LAKES! EVERYBODY SAYS SO!

And they're right!

No ban on fishing actually stops fishing. It just stops law-abiding folks. A ban shuts out the very people who would do the least harm, the very people who would help us take care of the place. It punishes the most innocent.

In a magazine I once described our closed watersheds as playgrounds for poachers and vandals. That's true because **poachers and vandals simply have a hard time getting away with much in public areas where honest sportsmen can see and report them.** They prey on watersheds because so few people are there to see them, and running from caretakers has become a sport in itself.

Every watershed manager has a collection of horror stories, stories that make them bitter and apprehensive. Yet in a way, their experience has been shaped by their own rules. **"No Trespassing" sets up a social filter. You shut out the Girl Scouts and wind up with outlaws.**

Here's a non-fishing example. Colorado's Florissant Fossil Beds National Monument has valuable fossils on the ground. Any 12-year-old might be tempted to pocket one. By one theory, it would be foolish to let the public anywhere near this national treasure. Even if only a tiny percentage of visitors had theft in mind, thousands of visitors would mean lots of thieves.

Yet the Park Service knows that visitors get fiercely protective. In practice, thousands of visitors mean thousands of guards, the more the better. The last time somebody tried to steal fossils, two different groups of visitors ran to report them. Indeed, the only trouble they've had with poachers, for example, is at night when the park is closed to the public.

Closure provides secrecy.

One Colorado Springs caretaker was fired and prosecuted for poaching elk and selling the meat, so even our watchmen sometimes need watching.

Since the publicity about opening the North Slope on Pikes Peak, committee members have been hearing confessions from all kinds of neighbors who are sick of fence-hopping. **Not every trespasser is a vandal or a poacher.** Some even release their catch. You can call that dropping the evidence, if you want, but they called it catch-and-release. They feel they were doing no harm. They want to help take care of the place.

Walk the shores of forbidden lakes (with a permit) and you'll find fishing litter—wads of line, bait containers—I even found a rod and reel complete with spinner. In some places, illegal anglers have worn paths in the ground!

Nobody can say these lakes aren't being fished (with the possible exception of Boulder's Iron Curtain country).

So if the lakes are being fished anyway, what would be the harm in allowing us law-abiding folks to join the fun? That is the 24-karat question. The lack of a good and clear answer has raised all kinds of suspicions. Because when people can't think of a good answer, they tend to think of a bad answer.

Did you hear the joke about the fisherman who was hauled into court for fishing a closed watershed? The judge got really mad and gave him a stern lecture: "And not only did you endanger our drinking water by dragging your filthy, hand-tied fly across it, but you were fishing my favorite spot!"

The public is convinced that closed reservoirs are actually open to public officials, but we are told this is no longer true. In the old days, it certainly was true! But in most communities, those days are supposed to be fading.

Still, there are exceptions, places where old rules and attitudes persist. Without hard evidence—photos, video, sworn testimony—any responsible journalist can only report the official denials, but it is also true that official denials are widely disbelieved by local anglers. In fact, the rumor is almost as damaging as proof because it makes people just as mad. Wherever policies seem to make no sense, that old suspicion will persist.

That suspicion—that reservoirs remain closed to the public because they are actually private fishing holes for the powerful and the privileged—is a deep and painful wound in Colorado, a wound that won't properly heal until everybody is

sure that everybody enjoys the same rights. That can't happen until forbidden lakes open. People won't believe it otherwise.

And why should they?

Imagine the rewards for officials who open lakes. Instead of having people grumble behind their backs, officials who oversee open reservoirs bask in good will and great publicity. And besides, they can still fish there any time they want!

Many abuses tend to be low-level, guys with pickup trucks and keys who sneak in without the boss knowing. "Some of us have been sneaking in for years,"one such employee told me. "The fishing's great, but you know, for me it's going to be even more fun when it opens because I'll be able to bring my friends and family, my guests from out of town. Sharing will be more fun than sneaking in ever was."

Some cities have a very firm policy. If any city employee, no matter how high, is caught fishing a closed reservoir, that employee is supposed to be dismissed and prosecuted as an ordinary trespasser. The DOW reports that even a caretaker's children have been ticketed.

High-up officials have a lot to lose. They earn good salaries and can afford fishing trips to great locations elsewhere. And, frankly, some of them have not enjoyed good publicity on other issues and have reason to fear that the press and opponents might relish catching them in an embarrassing situation. So for them, the only solution is to proceed toward opening the lakes. Nothing short of that will quell the rumors and suspicion.

That said, there is another form of abuse that has legal sanction. Some cities create the illusion of opening by leasing exclusive fishing rights to special groups—often for a nominal sum. It has to be a select group. If they wanted to let just anybody in, that would amount to public fishing on public waters. So the whole idea of these lease arrangements is to provide special favors for a special class, an air of privilege, and that's the kind of air that a lot of Americans don't like the smell of. Should we be surprised when officials who grant these favors wind up sharing the privilege?

Ask yourself: When you spend your vacation dollars going to some American destination, don't you expect to be welcome on that city's public property? Wouldn't you feel snubbed to discover that only an elite group of locals could enjoy the public domain? And what are the economic consequences of snubbing tourists?

How many millions does a "No Trespassing" sign really cost?

From a practical point of view, it is time to forget the past and look forward to a better future. We can't afford to hold grudges against people who may have done what we all want to do.

SO WHAT NEEDS TO BE DONE?

Imagine a city somewhere else that dreams of providing a fishing lake for its citizens and tourists. Imagine the problem!

First of all, there would have to be a lot of political support, campaigning, jaw-boning, maybe even an election. Then there would be the legal hassles, the necessary environmental studies, site selection, land aquisition. Just raising the money would be a huge project in itself. And then would come the construction phase, attacking the earth with explosives and heavy equipment. In the end, that city would be lucky if their years of work and tons of money resulted in anything as beautiful as the lakes that already await us in the Colorado Rockies.

We're lucky. Our lakes already exist. All that work is done. Our biggest task is changing our minds.

Some cities are still reluctant to experiment, but the good news is that major cities are leading the way and are happy with their experiments. **Officials from Denver, Aurora and Colorado Springs describe the success of lake openings with great pride. They've tried on the white hat and like it very much.**

It's working, but we all need to encourage Park and Rec. departments to get more involved. Fishermen don't need the elaborate facilities so often offered by these departments, but quite a few lakes remain closed for lack of any recreational management at all. **Just how much could it cost to stop arresting people?**

Some areas will require more work than others. Some projects will take years. Reluctant officials see themselves as prudent and cautious. They need our encouragement, and we need to help solve problems instead of throwing tantrums.

WHERE DOES THE DIVISION OF WILDLIFE STAND?

Individual cities may own their reservoirs, but except where unusual stocking has been done, the DOW owns their fish because wild fish are wildlife.

The DOW can't force a city to open a reservoir, but they can't actually take "no" for an answer either. At least, they can't take a once-and-for-all "no" for an answer. Because the division has a mandate under law to actively seek new fishing opportunities on public land. For the DOW, the issue never dies. They are required by law to keep trying. They're polite. They don't twist arms. When told "no," they go away politely, but they always come back later to ask again.

That's the law.

Best of all, the DOW comes offering money! Lots of recreation groups lobby local governments, wanting this or that, but few come bearing cash to pay for their projects. **The DOW offers three-to-one matching funds under their Fishing Is Fun program (three state dollars for every city dollar) and they sometimes have capital improvement funds that don't need matching at all. The DOW talks softly, but carries a big checkbook!**

None of this is ordinary tax money. That is, the old lady down the street who never goes fishing doesn't have to support DOW projects with her tax money. Instead, the DOW raises most of its funds by selling licenses. The only "tax" money they receive is from a small federal tax that is levied against the sale of sporting goods and boat gasoline. **All in all, sportsmen pay their own way.**

The DOW can't buy picnic tables, for example, because they aren't fishing related, but they can provide fishing trails, fish-cleaning stations, liability insurance, access road improvements, litter barrels and restrooms near the water, including the hauling of trash and sewage, and, of course, they always pay for stocking lakes with fish over and over again.

What a deal for local governments!

In fact, a number of local governments we contacted were actually surprised to learn that the DOW pays for so much. They were under the mistaken impression that they would have to buy stocker fish with city funds as a continuing expense.

Given the division's required persistence and tempting funds—and the enormous popularity of fishing—closed reservoirs probably can't remain closed forever. (Though it may seem like forever to anxious anglers.)

It is bound to be a step-by-step process, however, because the DOW's checkbook isn't big enough to handle a rush of new projects. If all the cities moved to open their waters all at once, the division couldn't handle it. Yet the sport is growing and so are license sales, so the trend is clear.

The division would also like to point out that wildlife management works, and lack of management does not necessarily result in whale-sized fish. **Too many anglers have the idea that closed reservoirs harbor huge fish. They may—by sheer luck—but if something goes wrong, there is no one to fix it. Some closed reservoirs actually have stunted fish, rather than whoppers, due to overpopulation. Fishing and fish management will actually improve our lakes for the benefit of all.**

TREAD SOFTLY: YOU'RE MAKING HISTORY

If anglers want to expand their freedoms on public lands, they need to be on their best behavior. You have to be as considerate as you possibly can to win the hearts and minds of reluctant water managers. If they can't tell you've been there, you might be welcome back and might have a new place to fish next summer.

Carry out the trash, even if it's not yours. Use the restrooms. If you're too far away from a restroom (it can be two miles in one spot I know), go as high and as far away from the water as you can and do it right in the minimum impact way. Make sure it's all buried in the top several inches of soil, the biological layer, where nature can take care of it quickly. I put a rock on the spot so no rainstorm can uncover the toilet paper. Appearance is just as important as the biology to water managers.

Be quiet. You can listen to music at home. If you bring it along, somebody may wonder if your equipment floats.

Leave your dog at home, even if they're allowed. Insist that your kids behave, too. Correct anybody who's smaller than you are. A lot of people respond to peer pressure.

If you see anybody busting the law or taking too much, report them. Operation Game Thief does not require your name or testimony, but they do pay rewards. Get the best description you can, licensed plate numbers, make of vehicle, description of clothing, anything. Then call 1-800-332-4155 toll free or in Denver call 295-0164. Your tip may not get them caught this time, but may help establish a pattern that will catch them next time.

And please use the trails. A trail is actually a narrow path of ruin designed to keep the surrounding area from being ruined.

Fisherman's trails have a bad reputation for developing into a lacework, and shortcutting switchbacks or big-footing down loose embankments causes huge ruts. Your dainty foot may not seem to do much harm at the time, but a rainstorm can turn your new tracks into an erosion problem, which spoils the shore and muddies the water and makes water managers pull their hair.

Beyond that, just try to obey the rules. If you object to your city's closures, write or call your City Council or utility department: Don't sneak in. It could cost you more than just a fine.

Manitou Springs, for example, threatens a fine of $1,000 and/or 90 days in jail. And Victor reminded us that they'll prosecute you for anything they can, which means stacking charges.

We thought we might tell you exactly what you could face for sneaking into a closed watersheds, but one prosecutor laughed, "Did you really think the law was going to be simple?"

You see, trespass has many degrees, depending upon the situation, and that's only the beginning. Fishing closed waters is an additional charge, and putting fish on a stringer is some kind of stealing. Did the caretaker find a sign damaged? Maybe you're a vandal, too. Never mind your story about climbing over the gate: If there's a fence cut somewhere, you're the one they caught inside. Has a lock or gate been broken? That might be criminal mischief or breaking and entering. And did you go along quietly or run? Did you resist arrest? Or assault an officer?

One thing is for sure. All this complication will drive your legal fees up.

Why not help to open these lakes to everyone instead of shutting yourself in jail? Here are some phone numbers:

Denver Water Board: (303) 628-6000
Aurora's Mayor (303) 695-7015.
Boulder's Mayor (303) 441-3002
Palmer Lake's Mayor (719) 481-2953.
Colo. Spgs. Water Op. Mgr. (719) 636-5616
Manitou Springs Mayor (719) 685-5481.
Cripple Creek's Mayor (719) 689-2502
Victor's Mayor (719) 689-2189.

REWARD

ONE MILLION ACRES OF
FREE CAMPING AND FUN RECREATION
IN DENVER'S CLOSEST
NATIONAL FOREST

CAPTURE TROUT IN REMOTE STREAMS, BEAVER PONDS AND IN MOUNTAIN LAKES STOCKED BY AIRCRAFT

HIKE, MOUNTAIN BIKE, RIDE HORSEBACK, AND CROSS-COUNTRY SKI WITH NO FEES! ALL SO CLOSE THAT YOU CAN SEE THE AREA FROM DOWNTOWN DENVER

Discover the sources of the river that flows through Denver.

Try the

TRAILS GUIDE TO PIKES PEAK COUNTRY

WHAT OTHERS ARE SAYING

"I liked it!" —Ed Dentry, Rocky Mtn. News Outdoor Writer

"Malocsay is a tireless campaigner for making the public domain public. His book will be useful as a an intriguing guide to what is and what might be."
—Karl Licis, Gazette Telegraph Outdoor Writer

"If it's possible to be an expert on lakes that aren't open to fishing, Zoltan Malocsay is it. No, he doesn't trespass or poach. He just makes a very convincing argument for opening now-closed public utility waters to public fishing—and how to get it done! He tells us where these forbidden jewels are and what they hold."
—Bob Saile, Denver Post Outdoor Writer

"Zoltan has done it again! First a usable trails guide that could be trusted. Now, a look into the myths and realities associated with our front range watersheds. A touch of history, flavored with a large dose of reality, provides the reader with insight into the foibles that govern public access to Colorado's mountain reservoirs. Here we have history, public health and guide book in one handy volume. *Opening Forbidden Lakes* is a great reference for the outdoor enthusiast."
—Paul Homan, Pikes Peak/Cheyenne
Mountain Journal Freelancer

"*Opening Forbidden Lakes* is a spirited book that guides, teaches and entertains; its ecological thinking is current and necessary."
—Will Hochman, Sierra Club Member